'Lord... Thou Saidst'

The Revelation of the Scriptures and the Testimony of Church History regarding the Intimate and Vital Relationship between God's Word and Prayer

Compiled by
Ray Graver

Living Stream Ministry
Anaheim, California • www.lsm.org

First Edition, March 1981.

ISBN 0-87083-046-5

Published by

Living Stream Ministry
2431 W. La Palma Ave., Anaheim, CA 92801 U.S.A.
P. O. Box 2121, Anaheim, CA 92814 U.S.A.

Printed in the United States of America

01   02   03   04   05   06   /   11   10   9   8   7   6   5   4   3

TABLE OF CONTENTS

FOREWORD

The psalmist declared, "How sweet are thy words unto my taste! yea, sweeter than honey to my mouth" (Psa. 119:103). How encouraging is the memory of the day when I first "tasted" the word of God. Often before that day I had studied, discussed, and memorized the Bible. But that day it was different. While reading in Acts, the words "that they had been with Jesus" (4:13) stood out. Soon the whole verse was alive. I read the words; I prayed the words; I sang the words; I went to the woods behind the dorm and shouted the words, "Unlearned and ignorant but they had been with Jesus! With Jesus! Oh, with Jesus!" Even now, some twenty years later, there is still the longing and the prayer to be one who has "been with Jesus." "Thy words were found, and I did eat them; and thy word was unto me the joy and rejoicing of mine heart" (Jer. 15:16). But the joy does not end there. How marvelous it is that today in the church life we are learning to exercise our spirit to feed upon the word of God. The word is truly living as we mingle our reading with prayer and our prayer with reading.

The quotations on the following pages show that many throughout the centuries have made this same discovery. Because it is impossible to convey the full context of each quotation, a list of references is furnished at the end of each chapter. It is our sincere longing that all of the Lord's children would learn to receive the word of God by means of all prayer (Eph. 6:17-18).

Houston, Texas
February 1981
Ray Graver

Unless otherwise noted, scriptures are quoted
from the King James Version.

Roman numerals in quotations
have been translated into Arabic numbers.

OUTLINE

I. The Revelation of the Scriptures
   A. The Word and Prayer
   B. The Testimony of the Old Testament Practice
      1. Jacob
      2. Moses
      3. David
      4. Solomon
      5. Daniel
      6. Ezra
      7. Nehemiah
   C. The Testimony of the New Testament Practice
      1. The Lord Jesus
      2. The Church in Jerusalem
      3. Paul
II. The Record of Church History
   A. The Testimony of the Early Church Writers
      1. Tertullian
      2. Origen
      3. Athanasius
      4. Jerome
      5. Ambrose
      6. Augustine
   B. The Testimony of the Early Reformers
      1. Martin Luther
      2. Philip Melanchthon
      3. William Tyndale
      4. Johann Heinreich Bullinger
      5. John Calvin
   C. The Testimony of the Puritans
      1. William Perkins
      2. Thomas Manton
      3. John Bunyan

D. The Testimony of the Pietists
1. Philip Jacob Spener
2. August Hermann Francke
E. The Testimony of the Evangelists
1. John Wesley
2. George Whitefield
3. Jonathan Edwards
F. The Testimony of the Missionaries
1. David Brainerd
2. Henry Martyn
3. Hudson Taylor
4. John Hyde
G. The Testimony of the Inner-life Writers
1. William Law
2. Andrew Murray
3. Hannah Whitall Smith
H. The Testimony of the Brethren
1. John Nelson Darby
2. George Müller
3. C. H. Mackintosh
I. The Testimony of the Evangelical Writers
1. Edward Bickersteth
2. Charles G. Finney
3. Andrew Bonar
4. Robert Murray McCheyne
5. Robert Govett
6. Joseph Barber Lightfoot
7. Brooke Foss Westcott
8. Charles Haddon Spurgeon
9. Edward M. Bounds
10. Alexander Whyte
11. Dwight L. Moody
12. Arthur T. Pierson
13. F. B. Meyer
14. Handley C. G. Moule
15. A. B. Simpson
16. Rueben A. Torrey
17. James M. Gray
18. S. D. Gordon

I. THE REVELATION OF THE SCRIPTURES (1)

A. The Word and Prayer

In every age and in every generation, the Lord has had His faithful servants to receive Him, to love Him, to proclaim Him, and to follow His way. Such men have always been characterized by a personal and intimate relationship with the Lord, an insight into His Word, and the grace to speak forth His truth. As we examine the lives and writings of these faithful ones, it is evident that their usefulness, their vitality, and their insight issued directly from personal, consecrated times of handling God's Word by prayer. They had discovered the intimate and vital relationship between God's Word and prayer.

For example, Martin Luther "spent a part of almost every day reading the Psalms, with which he mingled his own supplications amid tears and groans."[1] George Whitefield's vigorous gospel preaching came out of a daily habit of spending hours kneeling and reading and praying over the Scriptures.[2] R. A. Torrey considered it one of the rarest privileges of his life to read every chapter and every verse of the Bible on his knees.[3] Surely a clear realization of this relationship between the Word of God and prayer is basic to our Christian life and practice. "The vital connection between the word and prayer," wrote Andrew Murray, "is one of the simplest and earliest lessons of the Christian life."[4]

This relationship between the Word of God and prayer is twofold. On one hand, the key to the Word of God is prayer; on the other hand, the secret of prayer is the Word of God. By prayer, the Scriptures become a source of life, light, and nourishment.* By the Word of God our prayers are enriched,

*See note A, page 105.

strengthened, and established. These two portions from *The Necessity of Prayer* by E. M. Bounds point out both sides of the relationship:

> The Word of God is the food, by which prayer is nourished and made strong.[5]

> The Word of God is made effectual and operative, by the process and practice of prayer.[6]

Even as we review this twofold relationship revealed in the record of the Scriptures and confirmed in the biographies, journals, letters, and writings from church history, may we give ourselves freshly to times of praying and reading, and reading and praying, to times of pray-reading* God's holy Word.

As we take God's Word by prayer, we are enlivened and enlightened. As we saturate our prayers with God's Word, our petitions are uplifted and empowered. Both aspects of this intimate connection between God's Word and prayer are clearly revealed in the Scriptures. W. H. Griffith Thomas wrote in *Life Abiding and Abounding:*

> Thus the Word and Prayer are never absent from our life, and never far apart from each other. In the life of Old Testament believers they were always connected (Psa. 19; 119). In the life of our Lord they are constantly found together (John 17). In the life of the Early Church they are united (Acts 4:24-25; 6:4). In relation to the Holy Spirit they are inseparably connected (Eph. 6:17-18). There is not a single channel of belief, not a single element of experience, not a single pathway of service, not a single privilege, not a single grace, not a single hope, not a single possibility which is not in some way associated with the Word and Prayer. When these two are allowed to occupy in our life the place they occupy in God's purpose and plan for us, we have learnt the essential conditions, the blessed secret, the unspeakable joy of abiding in Christ and abounding for Christ.[7]

*See note D, page 111.

In addition to verses directly linking the Word to prayer, there is the clear testimony of the prayers recorded in both the Old and New Testaments. These prayers are prayers saturated with the words that the Lord had spoken to His people.

B. The Testimony of the Old Testament Practice

In the Old Testament, the revelation of prayer is mainly not by instruction but by example, and the prayers recorded there clearly point to the interdependence between the words that God had spoken and the words uttered in prayer. The words previously spoken by the Lord became the foundation, the basis, and even the content of the prayers of the Old Testament saints. A. W. Pink recognized this relationship and showed that the Lord's promises in the Scriptures were the substance of many of the prayers recorded in the Old Testament:

> Thus we are to lay hold of His pledged assurances, spread them before Him, and say, "Do as thou hast said" (2 Samuel 7:25). Observe how Jacob pleaded the promise in Genesis 32:12; Moses in Exodus 32:13; David in Psalm 119:58; Solomon in I Kings 8:25; and do thou, my Christian reader, likewise.[8]

Andrew Murray wrote in much the same way. He also pointed to the prayers recorded in the Old Testament to confirm the connection between God's words and our prayer:

> How well the Old Testament saints understood this connection between God's words and ours, and how

---

What God spake in promise was the root and the life of what they spake in prayer.

---

really prayer with them was the loving response to what they had heard God speak! If the word were a promise, they counted *on God to do as He had spoken.* "Do as Thou hast said;" "For Thou, Lord, hast spoken it;" "According to Thy promise!" "According to Thy word;" in such expressions they showed that what God spake in promise was the root and the life of what they spake in prayer.[9]

1. JACOB

The prayer of Jacob as recorded in Genesis 32:9-12 is one of the earliest prayers recorded in the Scriptures. Luther referred to it as "a beautiful specimen of all hearty prayer."[10] The prayer begins with Jacob calling upon the God of his forefathers and addressing Him as "the Lord which saidst unto

The Lord
which saidst unto me.

me," and it continues with his praying the very words which the Lord had previously spoken to him. God's Word was mingled with his prayer:

And Jacob said, O God of my father Abraham, and God of my father Isaac, the Lord which saidst unto me, Return unto thy country, and to thy kindred. (Gen. 32:9; cf. 31:13)

Jacob then confessed to the Lord his unworthiness and petitioned for deliverance from Esau. He concluded his prayer with "Thou saidst," and again he spoke back to the Lord the promises which the Lord had originally spoken to him:

And thou saidst, I will surely do thee good, and make thy seed as the sand of the sea, which cannot be numbered for multitude. (Gen. 32:12; cf. 28:14; 22:17)

Calling attention to this prayer of Jacob, Matthew Henry (1632—1714) in his exposition of the Old Testament emphasized the significance of God's Word in the practice of prayer:

The best we can say to God in prayer is what he has said to us. God's promises, as they are the surest guide of our desires in prayer, and furnish us with the best petitions, so they are the firmest ground of our hopes, and furnish us with the best pleas. "Lord, thou saidst thus and thus; and wilt thou not be as good as thy word, the word upon which thou hast *caused me to hope?*"[11]

C. H. Spurgeon also pointed to Jacob's use of the Lord's own words:

Now, the two pleas which Jacob used were God's precept and God's promise. First, he said, "Thou saidst unto me, Return unto thy country and to thy kindred": as much as if he put it thus:—"Lord, I am in difficulty, but I have come here through obedience to thee. Thou didst tell me to do this; now, since thou commandest me to come hither, into the very teeth of my brother Esau, who comes to meet me like a lion, Lord, Thou canst not be so unfaithful as to bring me into danger and then leave me in it." This was sound reasoning, and it prevailed with God. Then Jacob also urged a promise: "Thou saidst, I will surely do thee good."

Among men, it is a masterly way of reasoning when you can challenge your opponent with his own words: you may quote other authorities, and he may say, "I deny their force"; but, when you quote a man against himself, you foil him completely. When you bring a man's promise to his mind, he must either confess himself to be unfaithful and changeable, or, if he holds to being the same, and being true to his word, you have him, and you have won your will of him.[12]

2. MOSES

Moses, like Jacob, knew the Lord as One who had spoken, and he prayed according to that speaking adding the Lord's words to his own in prayer. After the children of Israel made the golden calf at the foot of the mount of God, Moses was bold in prayer:

> Remember Abraham, Isaac, and Israel, thy ser-
> vants, to whom thou swarest by thine own self, and
> saidst unto them, I will multiply your seed as the
> stars of heaven, and all this land that I have spo-
> ken of will I give unto your seed, and they shall
> inherit it for ever. (Exo. 32:13)

The Lord had spoken to Abraham (Gen. 12:7; 13:15;
15:7, 18), Isaac (26:4), and Jacob (28:13; 35:12), and that
speaking was later blent with this prayer of Moses. Such
a petition, strengthened with the Lord's words, prevented
the Lord from consuming the children of Israel.

Another significant prayer of Moses is recorded after the
children of Israel shrank back from entering into the good
land. This plea for the Lord to pardon the people was also
strengthened and established by the Lord's own words. First
Moses addressed the Lord, acknowledging Him as the One
who had spoken:

> And now, I beseech thee, let the power of my Lord
> be great, according as thou hast spoken saying...
> (Num. 14:17)

...as thou hast spoken saying...

He then prayed using the words spoken by the Lord as
recorded in Exodus 34:6-7 as part of his prayer:

> The Lord is long-suffering, and of great mercy, for-
> giving iniquity and transgression, and by no means
> clearing the guilty, visiting the iniquity of the fa-
> thers upon the children unto the third and fourth
> generation. (Num. 14:18; cf. Exo. 34:6-7)

Moses prayed according to the Lord's speaking, and the
Lord pardoned according to that prayer of Moses:

> And the Lord said, I have pardoned according to
> thy word. (Num. 14:20)

3. DAVID

The Lord's promises to David, conveyed by Nathan the

prophet, constrained and impelled him to pray. David's prayer as recorded in 2 Samuel 7 is rich with utterances displaying his reliance upon God's Word. Strengthened with such expressions as "but thou hast spoken," "For thy word's sake," "thy words be true," and "thou hast promised," he boldly turned

...and do as thou hast said.

God's promises into prayer. The essence of his prayer was what the Lord had spoken. This can be seen in verse 25:

> And now, O Lord God, the word that thou hast spoken concerning thy servant, and concerning his house, establish it for ever, and do as thou hast said. (2 Sam. 7:25)

C. H. Spurgeon reflected on these words of David, "Do as thou hast said," and pointed them to the "best praying in all the world":

> You put your finger down upon the very lines, and say, "Do as thou hast said." This is the best praying in all the world. O beloved, be filled with God's Word.[13]

The Scottish reformer, John Knox (1505—1572) used this prayer of David as an example of prayer based on God's promise:

> For his Gracious Majestie estemeth not the prayer, nether granteth the petitioun for any dignitie of the persone that prayith, but for his promeis sake onlie; and thairfoir sayith David, "Thou hes promeisit unto thy servand, O Lord, that thow wilt build a house for him, whairfoir thy servand hath found in his hart to pray in thy sycht, now evin so, O Lord, thou art God, and thy wordis ar trew: Thow hes spokin theis thingis unto thy servand, begyn thairfoir to do according to thy promeis; multiplie, O Lord, the houshald of thy servand."[14]

4. SOLOMON

The long prayer of Solomon after the building of the temple is constituted primarily with quotations and allusions to the Lord's Word recorded in Leviticus and Deuteronomy and includes direct references to the words spoken by the Lord to Moses and to David. Solomon's reliance upon the Lord's word to David is recorded in 1 Kings 8:25-26:

> Therefore now, Lord God of Israel, keep with thy servant David my father that thou promisedst him, saying, There shall not fail thee a man in my sight to sit on the throne of Israel. (v. 25)

> And now, O God of Israel, let thy word, I pray thee, be verified, which thou spakest unto thy servant David my father. (v. 26)

Keep...that thou promisedst him, saying...

The following extracts from Keil and Delitzsch's *Biblical Commentary on the Old Testament* indicate Solomon's strong dependence upon the Lord's Word for the content of the prayer:

> The substance of the prayer is closely connected with the prayer of Moses, especially with the blessings and curses therein. (*vid.* Lev. 26 and Deut. 28)[15]

> "Who keepeth covenant and mercy" [1 Kings 8:23], *verbatim* the same as in Deut. 7:9.[16]

> The prayer [1 Kings 8:31-32] refers to the cases mentioned in Ex. 22:6-12.[17]

> The following cases [1 Kings 8:33-53] are all taken from Lev. 26 and Deut. 28.[18]

> —refers to the threatenings in Lev. 26:17 and Deut. 28:25.[19]

Solomon had the threat in Lev. 26:33 and 44 in his eye.[20]

The plea "for they are Thy people," etc. (ver. 51), is taken from Deut. 4:10; and that in ver. 53, "Thou didst separate them," etc., is taken from Lev. 20:24, 26.[21]

"As Thou spakest by Moses" [1 Kings 8:53] points back to Ex. 19:5.[22]

Such prayer, intermingled with God's speaking, drew a clear response from the Lord (see 1 Kings 9:3-9). C. H. Spurgeon pointed out that such prayer based upon the Word touches God's honor:

> Solomon, at the opening of the temple, used this same mighty plea. He pleads with God to remember the word which He had spoken to [his] father David, and to bless that place. When a man gives a promissory note his honour is engaged. He signs his hand, and he must discharge it when the due time comes, or else he loses credit.[23]

5. DANIEL

Daniel, a faithful servant of the Lord, spent much time in prayer and in God's Word for enlightenment and insight. He gives this account of the background for his earnest prayer of confession:

> In the first year of his reign, I Daniel understood by the books the number of the years, whereof the word of the Lord came to Jeremiah the prophet. (Dan. 9:2)

When he set his face to pray, he freely mingled what he had read in "the books" with his prayer:

> And I prayed unto the Lord my God, and made my confession, and said, O Lord, the great and dreadful God, keeping the covenant and mercy to them that love him, and to them that keep his commandments. (v. 4)

Daniel had a clear foundation for this prayer. C. F. Keil in his commentary points out that "the thought, 'great and dreadful God, keeping the covenant and mercy,' etc....has its roots in Deut. 7:21 and 9." "The expression (ver. 15), 'Thou hast brought Thy people forth out of the land of Egypt with a mighty hand,' has its origin in Deut. 7:8, 9:26, etc."[24]

The remainder of his appeal (Dan. 9:5-19) draws numerous phrases and expressions from the law of Moses:

...that is written in the law of Moses. (v. 11)

As it is written in the law of Moses... (v. 13)

This prayer, founded upon and enriched with God's Word, drew forth a clear response from the Lord (see Dan. 9:20-27).

6. EZRA

Ezra, being "a ready scribe of the law of Moses," had much material available for his prayer as recorded in Ezra 9:6-15. Sections of the prayer can be traced to Leviticus, Numbers, Deuteronomy, Psalms, Jeremiah, Lamentations, and Isaiah.

Which thou hast commanded by thy servants the prophets, saying...

R. A. Bowman supplies us with a description of part of this petition:

> The verses are a medley of scriptural bits quoted sometimes in slightly modified form from Deuteronomy (cf. 7:1, 3, 12; 23:6) and loosely joined by biblical allusions which, in one instance at least (vs. 11; cf. Lev. 18:21-30), represent a free adaptation of other biblical texts.[25]

Here are six representative portions from Ezra's prayer, which can easily be traced back to the portions listed beside them:

For our iniquities are increased over our head. (Ezra 9:6)	For mine iniquities are gone over mine head. (Psa. 38:4)

Which thou hast commanded by thy servants the prophets, saying, The land, unto which ye go to possess it... (Ezra 9:11)

When the Lord thy God shall bring thee into the land whither thou goest to possess it....In the land whither ye go to possess it... (Deut. 7:1; 6:1)

Now therefore give not your daughters unto their sons, neither take their daughters unto your sons. (Ezra 9:12)

Thy daughter thou shalt not give unto his son, nor his daughter shalt thou take unto thy son. (Deut. 7:3)

...that ye may be strong, and eat the good of the land. (Ezra 9:12)

If ye be willing and obedient, ye shall eat good of the land. (Isa. 1:19)

...nor seek their peace or their wealth for ever. (Ezra 9:12)

Thou shalt not seek their peace nor their prosperity all thy days for ever. (Deut. 23:6)

...and leave it for an inheritance to your children for ever (Ezra 9:12)

...that ye may possess this good land, and leave it for an inheritance for your children after you for ever. (1 Chron. 28:8)

Ezra was not ashamed to inlay his prayer with rich portions of God's Word.

7. NEHEMIAH

In one of his prayers, Nehemiah, a contemporary of Ezra, reminded the Lord of His promise to gather His scattered people and bring them back to the place where He had chosen

to put His name. Nehemiah established his prayer principally upon what the Lord had spoken to Moses:

> Remember, I beseech thee, the word that thou
> commandedst thy servant Moses, saying... (Neh.
> 1:8)

E. W. Hamrick found certain features of Nehemiah's
prayer especially noteworthy:

> Like the prayers in [Nehemiah] 9:6-37 and in
> Daniel 9:4-19, it is composed mostly of stereo-
> typed Deuteronomic phrases (cf. Deut. 7:9, 21;
> 9:29; 21:15; 30:1-5)[26]

The following excerpts from an exposition of this prayer
(Herbert E. Ryle, editor) illustrate Nehemiah's dependence
upon the Lord's written word for the content and strength of his
prayer:

And said, I beseech thee, O Lord God of heaven, the great and terrible God, that keepeth covenant and mercy for them that love him and observe his commandments. (Neh. 1:5)

...were very probably a recognised formula of prayer based on the language of Deuteronomy.[27]

...that keepeth covenant and mercy for them that love him and observe his commandments. (Neh. 1:5)

The sentence which is borrowed from Deut. 7:9...[28]

...though there were of you cast out unto the uttermost part of the heaven... (Neh. 1:9)

This and the next clauses are clearly taken from Deut. 30:4, where the same words...occur.[29]

...unto the place that I have chosen to set my name there. (Neh. 1:9)

In five of these passages ([Deut.] 12:11, 14:23, 16:6, 11, 26:2) the full phrase is found, "the place which the Lord thy God shall choose to cause his name to dwell there," which Nehemiah here quotes.[30]

...that thou commandedst thy servant Moses, saying...

REFERENCES

[1]Philip Melanchthon, "Melanchthon's Oration at the Funeral of Martin Luther," *Great Voices of the Reformation,* Harry Emerson Fosdick, ed. (New York: Random House, 1952), p. 134.

[2]Arnold A. Dallimore, *George Whitefield* (London: The Banner of Truth Trust, 1971), vol. 1, p. 265.

[3]R. A. Torrey, *The Importance and Value of Proper Bible Study* (Chicago, IL: Moody Press, 1921), p. 48.

[4]Andrew Murray, *With Christ in the School of Prayer* (New York: J. H. Sears & Company, 1885), p. 151.

[5]E. M. Bounds, *The Necessity of Prayer* (Grand Rapids, MI: Baker Book House, 1976), p. 123.

[6]*Ibid.,* p. 122.

[7]W. H. Griffith Thomas, *Life Abiding and Abounding* (Chicago, IL: The Bible Institute Colportage Association, n.d.), pp. 6-7.

[8]A. W. Pink, *Profiting from the Word* (Carlisle, PA: The Banner of Truth Trust, 1970), p. 100.

[9]Murray, *With Christ in the School of Prayer,* p. 154.

[10]Abraham Gosman, *Genesis;* German ed., John Peter Lange; English ed., T. Lewis and A. Gosman (New York: Charles Scribner's Sons, 1884), p. 333.

[11]Matthew Henry, *Matthew Henry's Commentary on the Whole Bible* (New York: Fleming H. Revell Company, 1925), vol. 1, p. 17.

[12]C. H. Spurgeon, *Twelve Sermons on Prayer* (Grand Rapids, MI: Baker Book House, 1971), p. 50.

[13]C. H. Spurgeon, *The Secret of Power in Prayer* (London: Metropolitan Tabernacle Pulpit, 1888, reprinted by Pilgrim Publications, Pasadena, TX), p. 21.

[14]John Knox, *The Works of John Knox,* ed. David Laing (New York: AMS Press Inc., 1966), vol. 3, p. 93.

[15]C. F. Keil, "The Books of the Kings," *Biblical Commentary on the Old Testament,* trans. James Martin (Grand Rapids, MI: Wm. B. Eerdmans Publishing Company, 1970), p. 125.

[16]*Ibid.,* p. 126.

[17]*Ibid.,* p. 128.

[18]*Ibid.,* p. 129.

[19]*Ibid.,* p. 129.

[20]*Ibid.,* p. 132.

[21]*Ibid.,* p. 133.

[22]*Ibid.,* p. 133.

[23]Spurgeon, *Twelve Sermons on Prayer,* p. 40.

[24]C. F. Keil, *Biblical Commentary on the Book of Daniel,* trans. M.G. Easton (Grand Rapids, MI: Wm. B. Eerdmans Publishing Company, 1968), p. 327.

[25]Raymond A. Bowman, "Ezra," *The Interpreter's Bible* (New York: Abingdon Press, 1954), vol. 3, p. 650.

[26]Emmett Willard Hamrick, "Ezra—Nehemiah; Commentary on the Text," *The Broadman Bible Commentary,* ed. Clifton J. Alien (Nashville, TN: Broadman Press, 1970), vol. 3, p. 472.

[27]Herbert Edward Ryle, ed., *The Books of Ezra & Nehemiah* (Cambridge: University Press, 1923), p. 151.

[28]*Ibid.,* p. 152.

[29]*Ibid.,* p. 154.

[30]*Ibid.,* p. 155.

CHAPTER TWO

I. THE REVELATION OF THE SCRIPTURES (2)

C. The Testimony of the New Testament Practice

The prayers recorded in the New Testament, like those in the Old Testament, clearly confirm the relationship between God's Word and prayer.

1. THE LORD JESUS

Andrew Murray and Bishop Horne have given clear utterance to their realization of the use made by our Lord of the Scripture in His prayers. In *The Prayer Life,* Murray prescribes the Word and prayer for a healthy and powerful spiritual life. Using the prayers of the Lord as an example, he indicates that the Word supplies the material for prayer:

> Think of the Lord Jesus. In His youth and manhood He treasured the Word in His heart. In the temptation in the wilderness, and on every opportunity that presented itself—till He cried out on the cross in death, "My God, my God, why hast thou forsaken me?" [Matt. 27:46 from Psa. 22:1] He showed that the Word of God filled His heart. And in His prayer life He manifested two things: first, that the Word supplies us with material for prayer and encourages us in expecting everything from God. The second is that it is only by prayer that we can live such a life that every word of God can be fulfilled in us.[1]

Bishop (George) Horne (1730—1792), in the preface to his commentary on the Psalms, emphatically relates the significance of the Lord's use of the Psalms in His prayers:

In the language of this Divine book, therefore, the prayers and praises of the Church have been offered up to the Throne of Grace, from age to age. And it appears to have been the Manual of the Son of God, in the days of his flesh...who pronounced on

...in the Psalmist's form of words rather than his own.

the Cross, the beginning of the 22d Psalm, "My God! my God! why hast thou forsaken me?"—and expired with a part of the 31st Psalm in his mouth, "Into thy hands I commend my spirit." Thus, he who had not the Spirit by measure, in whom were hidden all the treasures of wisdom and knowledge, and who spake as never man spake, yet chose to conclude his life, to solace himself in his greatest agony, and at last to breathe out his soul in the Psalmist's form of words rather than his own.[2]

2. THE CHURCH IN JERUSALEM

Two accounts in the book of Acts indicate that the believers in the church in Jerusalem practiced combining the Holy Word with their prayer. It is significant that these two accounts seem to include the only recorded prayers from the meetings of the believers in the New Testament.

The first account is in Acts 1. After the Lord's ascension the disciples gathered "with one accord in prayer" (v. 14). Acts 1:24 gives us a portion of the content of their prayer:

And they prayed, and said, Thou, Lord, which knowest the hearts of all men, show whether of these two thou hast chosen.

This short prayer was firmly rooted in the Word of God. Solomon had testified "for thou, *even* thou only, knowest the hearts of all the children of men" (1 Kings 8:39). So they prayed according to the Word, petitioning the Lord, and applying the Word to their need.

The second prayer is recorded in Acts 4:24-30. After Peter and John were released by the Sanhedrin, they returned to their own company and reported all that had happened. When the church had heard, "they lifted up their voice to God with one accord" (v. 24). The ensuing petitions by the church in Jerusalem were not words of mere human invention; rather, they prayed using divinely inspired words from the Scripture.

...a verbatim quote of the Septuagint text of Psalm 2:1-2.

First, they addressed the Lord in a praising way, using the words of Exodus 20:11:

> Lord, thou art God, which hast made heaven, and earth, and the sea, and all that in them is. (Acts 4:24 from Exo. 20:11)

The church then petitioned using "a verbatim quote of the Septuagint text of Psalm 2:1-2."[3]

> Who by the mouth of thy servant David hast said, Why did the heathen rage, and the people imagine vain things? The kings of the earth stood up, and the rulers were gathered together against the Lord, and against his Christ. (Acts 4:25-26 from Psa. 2:1-2)

The believers prayed these two Old Testament verses word for word from the Psalms. Continuing their prayer, "The words of the Psalm and those of the application are interwoven."[4] They applied these verses to their experience, specifying the name of Jesus as the anointed One and the names "Herod and Pontius Pilate" as "kings of the earth" and "rulers." The words of the Scripture were the foundation and content of their prayers.

3. PAUL

The apostle Paul also practiced using Scripture for the content and direction for his prayer. In Ephesians 1:17-23 Paul prayed for the saints to be enlightened as to their hope and inheritance and for their participation in the mighty power of God. Such power, he prayed, was:

> ...wrought in Christ, when he raised him from the dead, and set him at his own right hand in the heavenly places, far above all principality, and power, and might, and dominion, and every name that is named, not only in this world, but also in that which is to come: And hath put all things under his feet. (vv. 20-22)

This prayer, offered by one intimately familiar with the Old Testament, is framed in the thought and the language of the Psalms. Bishop Westcott in his notes on Ephesians designated Psalms 110 and 8 as the source of portions of the prayer:[5]

> The Lord said unto my Lord, Sit thou at my right hand, until I make thine enemies thy footstool. (Psa. 110:1)

> Thou madest him to have dominion over the works of thy hands: thou hast put all things under his feet. (Psa. 8:6)

Later Paul encouraged the believers to "take...the sword of the Spirit, which is [the] word of God, by means of all prayer and petition, praying at every time in spirit (Eph. 6:17)."[6] Concerning these verses Arno C. Gaebelein (1861—1945) wrote in *The Annotated Bible:*

> Prayer always with all prayer and supplication in the Spirit, is next to the sword of the Spirit the most powerful weapon against the devil and his wicked hosts. We must read the Word and pray.

Prayer and the Word cannot be separated.

Prayer and the Word cannot be separated. The searching of the Word must be done with prayer and prayer will be effectual through knowing the Word.[7]

In *The Path of Prayer* Samuel Chadwick uses Paul's words to show the link between the Word and prayer:

The Word of God quickens the soul and instructs it in prayer....St. Paul links together the Word of God and prayer. "And take...the sword of the Spirit which is the Word of God; praying always with all prayer and supplication, and watching thereunto with all perseverance and supplication for all saints; and for me." Watching where and whereunto? Watching with all perseverance! That is surely with diligence and patience, alertness and reverence. We must search the Word, that we may know how to pray.[8]

In *Effective Prayer* J. Oswald Sanders also wrote concerning Paul's exhortation:

What is our weapon? Our Leader has placed in our hands the irresistible sword of the Spirit which defeated the devil in the wilderness—the Word of God. But its aggressive and conquering power is released only through the prayer of faith. Our instructions are, "Take the sword of the Spirit...praying always with all prayer and supplication in the Spirit...with all perseverance." This is no mere passive praying. Only aggressive prayer based on the Word of God dislodges the enemy from his citadel.[9]

W. Graham Scroggie pointed to the same words in Ephesians 6:17-18 to show that God's Word to us and our word to Him must be vitally related in our practice:

What we need is a real vision of what prayer is, and such a vision will come to us only as we bring the Bible and our prayer-life into intimate relation. Too long have prayer and Bible study been divorced, and with sad results. What God has joined together, we

His Word to us, and our word to Him are vitally related in His purpose, and must be vitally related in our practice.

should never have put asunder. His word to us, and our word to Him are vitally related in His purpose, and must be vitally related in our practice. We are exhorted to "take the Sword of the Spirit, which is the Word of God, praying always with all prayer and supplication in the Spirit," and again, we read of what is "sanctified by the Word of God and prayer."[10]

REFERENCES

[1] Andrew Murray, *The Prayer Life* (Chicago, IL: Moody Press, n.d.), pp. 88-89.

[2] Church of England, *The Book of Psalms,* Bishop George Horne, "Extracts" (London: Samuel Hodgson, 1845), front piece.

[3] T. C. Smith, "Acts; Commentary on the Text," *The Broadman Bible Commentary,* ed. Clifton J. Alien (Nashville, TN: Broadman Press, 1970), vol. 10, p. 40.

[4] Gotthard Victor Lechler, *The Acts of the Apostles,* trans. and ed. Charles Schaeffer (New York: Charles Scribner's Sons, 1884), p. 79.

[5] Brooke Foss Westcott, *Saint Paul's Epistle to the Ephesians* (New York: Macmillian and Company, 1906; reprinted, Minneapolis, MN: Klock & Klock Christian Publishers, 1978), p. 200.

[6] Alfred Marshall, *The Interlinear Greek-English New Testament* (London: Samuel Bagster and Sons Limited, 1958), p. 775.

[7] Arno C. Gaebelein, *The Annotated Bible* (Chicago, IL: Moody Press and Loizeaux Brothers, 1970), vol. 3, p. 273.

[8] Samuel Chadwick, *The Path of Prayer* (Fort Washington, PA: Christian Literature Crusade, 1931), p. 27.

[9] J. Oswald Sanders, *Effective Prayer* (Chicago, IL: Moody Press, 1969), p. 36.

[10] W. Graham Scroggie, *Method in Prayer* (New York: Hodder and Stoughton, 1916), pp. 18-19.

CHAPTER THREE

II. THE RECORD OF CHURCH HISTORY (1)

Authority for truth and practice among the believers must rest solely upon the Word of God with any review of church history serving as confirmation and encouragement. As we have seen, there is the clear revelation in the Scriptures of the intimate relationship between God's Word and prayer. In the following sections it will become clear that there is also the strong confirmation of such a relationship in the pages of church history.

A. The Testimony of the Early Church Writers

The early records of church history include several writings that give a view into the early church practice. The letter *Clement to the Corinthians,* written near the close of the first century, concludes with a prayer "full of Scriptural reminiscences"[1] and "nourished with memories of the psalms, prophets, Gospels, and apostolic writings."[2] Phrase by phrase the Word of God was turned into prayer.

> Open the eyes of our hearts [cf. Eph. 1:18], that we may know Thee [cf. Phil. 3:10], who alone *abidest Highest in the lofty, Holy in the holy* [cf. Isa. 57:15]; who *layest low the insolence of the proud* [cf. Isa. 13:11], who *scatterest the imaginings of nations* [cf. Psa. 2:1, 9]; who *settest the lowly on high* [cf. Job 5:11], and *bringest the lofty low* [cf. Isa. 10:33]; who *makest rich and makest poor; who killest and makest alive* [cf. 1 Sam. 2:6-7];...*Let* all *the Gentiles know that Thou art God alone* [cf. 2 Kings 19:15], and Jesus Christ is Thy Son [cf. Matt. 3:17], and *we*

are Thy people and the sheep of Thy pasture [cf. Psa. 79:13].[3]

The second record is a letter from Pliny, a Roman provincial governor and a persecutor of the church, to the emperor Trajan in A.D. 105. Pliny described the gatherings of the early Christians in which they came together before daybreak to speak verses alternately among themselves to Christ as to God (*"quod essent soliti stato die ante lucem convenire carmenque Christo quasi deo dicere secum invicem"*).[4]

During the next four hundred years, the faith was preached and defended by those referred to as the early church fathers. The following excerpts from the writings of Tertullian, Origen, Athanasius, Jerome, Ambrose, and Augustine help to confirm that the early church fathers had a keen awareness of the interdependence of God's Word and prayer.

1. TERTULLIAN

Tertullian (160—220) of North Africa, a strong defender of the faith, was a prolific writer and an ardent preacher. In his treatise concerning prayer he wrote:

> Lest we should be as far away from the ears of God as we are from His precepts, the recollection of the precepts [such as Matt. 5:24] paves the way to heaven for our prayers.[5]

He encouraged the prayerful to bring to God what he called "enriched prayer."[6]

> The more diligent in prayer are wont to subjoin in their prayers the "Hallelujah" [Psa. 145—150] and such kind of psalms.[7]

2. ORIGEN

In the third century Origen (185—254) wrote commentaries covering nearly all the books of the Bible. He was described as a man whose "thought was nourished on Scripture, the inspiration and integrity of which he affirmed."[8] In his *Homily on Exodus* he pointed to the need for supplication when coming to the Word:

> Hence, it is shown that not only must study be applied by us in order to learn the Sacred Writings, but also supplication must be made to the Lord and we must beseech Him "day and night" [Josh. 1:8] that the Lamb "of the tribe of Judah" come and that He Himself taking the "sealed book" [Rev. 5:5] would deign to open it.[9]

In this way he testified that it is ultimately through prayer that the Lord has the way to unlock the holy Word for us. In his letter to Gregory, Origen charged him to "diligently apply [himself] to the reading of the sacred Scriptures."[10]

> And applying yourself thus to the divine study, seek aright, and with unwavering trust in God, the meaning of the holy Scriptures, which so many have missed. Be not satisfied with knocking and seeking; for prayer is of all things indispensable to the knowledge of the things of God. For to this the Saviour exhorted, and said not only, "Knock, and it shall be opened to you; and seek, and ye shall find," but also, "Ask, and it shall be given unto you."[11]

3. ATHANASIUS

Athanasius of Alexandria (296—372) was also a strong defender of the faith, writing vigorously against heresy and vindicating the deity of Christ. He encouraged the use of the Psalms for the wording of prayer.

Bring thy case before God in the words of the Psalms.

In this book thou findest the whole life of man pictured, the moods of the heart, the movements of the thoughts. If thou hast need of repentance, if thou hast met trial and temptation, if thou art exposed to

persecution and calumny, in all and in every case,
thou canst find here instruction, and bring thy case
before God in the words of the Psalms.[12]

4. JEROME

Jerome (340—420), best known for his two Latin transla-
tions of the Bible, encouraged the mingling of prayer with the
study of the Word:

> Let there be study of the Divine Word, mingled
> with prayer.[13]

5. AMBROSE

Ambrose (340—397), whose preaching led to the conver-
sion of Augustine, recommended the Scriptures as a source of
spiritual food:

Bruise and refine
the utterances
of the heavenly Scriptures.

We ought for a long while to bruise and refine the
utterances of the heavenly Scriptures, exerting our
whole mind and heart upon them, that the sap of
that spiritual food* may diffuse itself into all the
veins of our soul.[14]

6. AUGUSTINE

Perhaps the best known of the early church fathers was
Augustine (354—430). Dean (R. C.) Trench (1807—1886)
wrote of his "unquenched and unquenchable thirst for the
Word,"[15] and John Baillie commented that he who appreci-
ates aright the lesson of Augustine's life, will go, with a
deeper relish and on "bended knee" to the Word which was
his daily all.[16] His prayerful longing was to confess to the
Lord the entire Bible:

*See note A, page 105.

Let me confess unto Thee whatsoever I shall find
in Thy books, and hear the voice of praise, and
drink in Thee, and meditate* on the wonderful
things out of Thy law; even from the beginning,
wherein Thou madest the heaven and the earth,
unto the everlasting reigning of Thy holy city with
Thee.[17]

In one account he described how he "read, and kindled"
the words of a psalm. The words of the psalm became the
words of his prayer:

I read, and kindled.

—I read that verse—"I will both lay me down in
peace, and sleep; for Thou, Lord, only makest me
dwell in safety" [Psa. 4:8]; and, with a loud cry of
my heart, I cried out, O "in peace!" O for the
self-same! O, what said he, "I will lay me down and
sleep?" I read, and kindled.[18]

Augustine testified that in his experience prayer flowed forth
as he read the Psalms:

Oh! in what accents spake I unto Thee, my God,
when I read the Psalms of David.[19]

B. The Testimony of the Early Reformers

After a prolonged spiritual darkness during the Middle
Ages, light broke forth as the Lord raised up such men as
Luther, Tyndale, and Calvin to declare that His Word, not the
decrees and presumptions of men, is the supreme authority and
light for His people. To these reformers a continual and personal contact with the Word was crucial, and prayer, no longer a
mere ritual, became the vehicle for penetrating its depths.

1. MARTIN LUTHER

The German reformer, Martin Luther (1483—1546), related from his own experience his dependence upon the Word

*See note B, page 107.

of God for his prayer, and declared the need for prayer in the study of the Scriptures. In response to a request for a simple way to pray, he disclosed his own practice of combining the Word with prayer:

> Dear Master Peter: I will tell you as best I can what I do personally when I pray. May our dear Lord grant to you and to everybody to do it better than I! Amen.
>
> First, when I feel that I have become cool and joyless in prayer...I take my little psalter, hurry to my room...and, as time permits, I say quietly to myself and word-for-word the Ten Commandments,...some words of Christ or of Paul or some psalms, just as a child might do.[20]

Using the Lord's words in Matthew 6 as an example, he continued by showing his way of "elaborating each portion in a way to kindle fire in his heart"[21]:

> Then repeat one part or as much as you wish, perhaps the first petition: "Hallowed be thy name," and say: "Yes, Lord God, dear Father, hallowed be thy name, both in us and throughout the whole world."[22]

"With practice," Luther concluded, "one can take the Ten Commandments on one day, a psalm or chapter of Holy Scripture the next day, and use them as flint and steel to kindle a flame in the heart."[23]

In *A Treatise on Good Works* Luther encouraged the use of the Psalms as prayer:

> Here a man must make daily use of those prayers David prayed, "Lord, lead me in thy path, and let me not walk in my own ways" (Psalm 119:35, 37), and many like prayers, which are all summed up in the prayer, "Thy kingdom come."[24]

The following incident describes Luther's experience in a time of crisis. He prayed, weaving the Scriptures into his petition to God:

Appalled at the scene, he exclaimed: "O God, how has the devil injured this Thy instrument!" Then he went to the window and prayed. All the promises of the Holy Scriptures concerning answers to prayer that he could recall were repeated and woven into the prayer. This done, he turned to the bed, and grasped his friend by the hand with the words: "Be of good cheer, Philip, thou shalt not die!"[25]

Luther, who had learned the secret of mingling the Word with his prayer, also "always combined prayer with the study of the Word."[26] In 1518 he replied to a friend's inquiry regarding the best method of studying the Scriptures:

As yet, most excellent Spalatin, you have only asked me things that were in my power. But to direct you in the study of the Holy Scriptures is beyond my ability. If, however, you absolutely wish to know my method, I will not conceal it from you.

It is very certain, that we cannot attain to the understanding of Scripture either by study or by the intellect. Your first duty is to begin by prayer.[27]

He spent a part of almost every day reading the Psalms, with which he mingled his own supplications amid tears and groans.

Philip Melanchthon, a Greek scholar, spent many years working closely with Martin Luther. At Luther's funeral he testified of the reformer's practice of mingling prayer with the Word:

What shall I say of his other virtues? Often have I found him weeping and praying for the whole

church. He spent a part of almost every day reading the Psalms, with which he mingled his own
supplications amid tears and groans.[28]

2. PHILIP MELANCHTHON

Philip Melanchthon (1497—1560) was, like Luther, known
for his life of prayer. He believed that "true prayer is made
only by those who hear the Word."[29] Melanchthon and his
wife, both influenced no doubt by Luther, practiced using the
Word in prayer. In his old age he wrote concerning the death
of his wife:

> And so it is that I miss her everywhere. I remember
> how almost daily she repeated these words of the
> psalm, "Forsake me not in my old age" [Psa. 71:9].
> And thus I also continually pray.[30]

3. WILLIAM TYNDALE

William Tyndale's (1494—1536) love for the Word led him
to produce the first complete English translation of the Bible.
Such a scholar recommended prayer when coming to the
Scripture:

> Forasmuch then as the scripture is nothing else
> but that which the Spirit of God hath spoken by the
> prophets and apostles, and cannot be understood
> but of the same Spirit; let every man pray to God to
> send him his Spirit, to loose him from his natural
> blindness and ignorance, and to give him under-
> standing and feeling of the things of God, and of
> the speaking of the Spirit of God.[31]

4. JOHANN HEINREICH BULLINGER

Johann Heinreich Bullinger (1504—1575), the Swiss
reformer and successor to Huldrych Zwingli (1484—1531),
wrote concerning the need for prayer in handling the Scripture:

> And finally, the most effectual rule of all, whereby
> to expound the word of God, is an heart...which
> doth continually pray.[32]

5. JOHN CALVIN

John Calvin (1509—1564) was a primary figure in carrying out the Reformation in Switzerland as Luther did in Germany, seeking to restore the church to its original purity. In his lifelong work, *Institutes of the Christian Religion,* he pointed to the Word of God as the fuel for the believers' prayer:

Believers know by use and experience that ardor

The Word of God is the only sure foundation for prayer.

burns low unless they supply new fuel. Accordingly, among our prayers, meditation* both on God's nature and on his Word is by no means superfluous.[33]

Calvin fought against the practice of prayer made to dead saints and strongly maintained that prayer should be based on the Word of God:

But briefly to conclude this point, I take my stand on the declaration of Paul, that no prayer is genuine which springs not from faith, and that faith cometh by the Word of God. (Rom. 10:14.) In these words, he has, if I mistake not, distinctly intimated that the Word of God is the only sure foundation for prayer.[34]

*See note B, p. 107.

REFERENCES

[1]Jules Lebreton and Jacques Zeiller, *The History of the Primitive Church,* trans. Ernest C. Messenger (New York: The MacMillan Company, 1949), vol. 1, p. 458.

[2]*Ibid.,* p. 460.

[3]S. Clement of Rome, "Epistle to the Corinthians," J. B. Lightfoot, *The Apostolic Fathers,* ed. J. R. Harmer (Grand Rapids, MI: Baker Book House, 1976), pp. 38-39.

[4]Caecilius Secundus Plinius, *Pliny Letters,* trans. William Melmoth (Cambridge, MA: Harvard University Press, 1947), vol. 2, p. 402.

[5]Tertullian, "Concerning Prayer," *Tertullian's Treatises; Concerning Baptism,* trans. Alexander Souter (New York: The MacMillan Company, 1919), p. 28.

[6]Tertullian, "On Prayer," *The Ante-Nicene Fathers,* ed. Alexander Roberts and James Donaldson (Grand Rapids, MI: Wm. B. Eerdmans Publishing Company, 1976), vol. 6, p. 690.

[7]*Ibid.,* p. 690.

[8]*The Oxford Dictionary of the Christian Church,* ed. F. L. Cross and E .A. Livingston (London: Oxford University Press, 1974), p. 1009.

[9]Origen, *Origenes Werke.,* trans. unknown, Hrsg. im. Austrage der Kirchväter-Commission der Königl. Preussischen Akademie der Wissenschaften (Leipzig: J. C. Hinrichs, 1920), vol. 6, pp. 266-268.

[10]Origen, "A Letter from Origen to Gregory," *The Ante-Nicene Fathers,* ed. Alexander Roberts and James Donaldson (Buffalo, NY: The Christian Literature Publishing Company, 1885), vol. 4, p. 394.

[11]*Ibid.,* p. 394.

[12]Peter Ainslie, *The Way of Prayer* (New York: Fleming H. Revell Company, 1924), p. 106.

[13]Olive Wyon, *The School of Prayer* (Philadelphia, PA: The Westminister Press, 1944), p. 95.

[14]S. Ambrose, "De Abel et Cain, lib. ii. c. vi.," W. H. Hutchings, *The Life of Prayer* (London: Longmans, Green, and Co., 1897), p. 165.

[15]John Baillie, *St. Augustine: a Biographical Memoir* (New York: Robert Carter & Brothers, 1859), p. 8.

[16]*Ibid.,* p. 9.

[17]Augustine, *The Confessions of Saint Augustine,* trans. Edward B. Pusey (New York: Random House, 1949), p. 245.

[18]Baillie, p. 181.

[19]*Ibid.,* p. 169.

[20]Martin Luther, *Luther's Works, Devotional Writings II,* ed. Gustav K. Wiencke (Philadelphia, PA: Fortress Press, 1955), vol. 43, p. 193.

[21]*Ibid.,* p. 190.

[22]*Ibid.,* p. 195.

[23]*Ibid.,* p. 209.

[24]Martin Luther, *Luther's Works, the Christian in Society I,* ed. James Atkinson (Philadelphia, PA: Fortress Press, 1955), vol. 44, p. 73.

[25]Henry Eyster Jacobs, *Martin Luther, the Hero of the Reformation* (New York: G. P. Putnam's Sons, 1898), p. 336.

[26]Taylor G. Bunch, *Prevailing Prayer* (Washington, D. C.: Review and Herald, 1946), p. 46.

[27]J. H. Merle D'Aubigne, *History of the Reformation of the Sixteenth Century* (Grand Rapids, MI: Baker Book House, 1973), p. 106.

[28]Philip Melanchthon, "Melanchthon's Oration at the Funeral of Martin Luther," *Great Voices of the Reformation,* Harry Emerson Fosdick, ed. (New York: Random House, 1952), p. 134.

[29]Clyde Leonard Manschreck, *Melanchthon, the Quiet Reformer* (New York: Abingdon Press, 1958), p. 313.

[30]*Ibid.,* p. 315.

[31]William Tyndale, *Doctrinal Treatise and Introductions to Different Portions of the Holy Scriptures,* ed. Henry Walter (Cambridge: The University Press, 1848), pp. 88-89.

[32]Henry Bullinger, *The Decades of Henry Bullinger,* ed. Thomas Harding (Cambridge: The University Press, 1849), p. 79.

[33]John Calvin, *Calvin: Institutes of the Christian Religion,* ed. John T. McNeill (Philadelphia, PA: The Westminister Press, 1960), vol. 21, p. 867.

[34]John Calvin, *Tracts and Treatises on the Reformation of the Church,* trans. Henry Beveridge (Grand Rapids, MI: Wm. B. Eerdmans Publishing Company, 1958), vol. 1, p. 156.

CHAPTER FOUR

II. THE RECORD OF CHURCH HISTORY (2)

C. The Testimony of the Puritans

Reacting against the forms and rituals of the Roman Church and the newly established state churches, the Puritans came forth stressing a pure and strict habit of life.

Show Him His handwriting.

Separating themselves from both religious stagnation and popular amusements, they encouraged private and household Scripture reading and prayer.

1. WILLIAM PERKINS

At the beginning of the seventeenth century, the most influential Puritan writer was William Perkins (1558—1602). He proposed that those hearing the Word "must doe as the beast doth, fetch up the meate out of his bellie againe, and chewe it over a new. The man that doth so, is the fittest for the Lords use."[1] He maintained that in prayer:

> Every petition must be grounded upon the word of God, and not framed according to the carnall conceit and fansie of mans braine.[2]

2. THOMAS MANTON

Thomas Manton (1620—1677), another Puritan writer, suffered imprisonment because of his faithfulness to speak forth the truths of the Word. He also encouraged the use of God's Word in prayer:

> One way to get comfort is to plead the promise of

God in prayer, show Him His handwriting; God is
tender of His Word.[3]

3. JOHN BUNYAN

The Pilgrim's Progress, an allegory of the Christian life,
is acclaimed and esteemed by Christians throughout the
world. Its author, John Bunyan (1628—1688), in "A Discourse
Touching Prayer," shows how the Spirit enlivens and stirs up
the heart to "supplicate, according to the Word"[4]:

> Prayer it is, when it is within the compass of God's
> word; and it is blasphemy, or at best vain babbling,
> when the petition is beside the book. David therefore
> still, in his prayer, kept his eye on the word of God:
> "My soul," saith he, "cleaveth to the dust; quicken me
> according to thy word." (Ps. 119:25.) And again; "My
> soul melteth for heaviness: strengthen me according
> to thy word." (ver. 28.) And, "Remember thy word
> unto thy servant, on which thou hast caused me to
> hope." (ver. 49.)[5]

Bunyan's biographical article, *Grace Abounding to the
Chief of Sinners,* reveals that the Word was an ingredient in
his personal prayer life:

> But the next day at evening, being under many
> fears, I went to seek the Lord; and as I prayed I
> cried, and my soul cried to him in these words, with
> strong cries: "O Lord, I beseech thee show me that
> thou hast loved me with everlasting love." (Jer.
> 31:3.) I had no sooner said it, but with sweetness
> this returned upon me, as an echo, or sounding
> again, "I have loved thee with an everlasting love."
> Now I went to bed in quiet; also when I waked the
> next morning it was fresh upon my soul, and I be-
> lieved it.[6]

D. The Testimony of the Pietists

The Pietist movement in Germany, drawing extensively
upon the writings of the Puritans, was a reaction against the
deadness and objective scholasticism of the state church.

Among the Pietists much attention was given to having a life of devotion and piety. The chief instruments for such a life were the reading of the Bible and daily prayer.

1. PHILIP JACOB SPENER

In 1675 German Pietist, Philip Jacob Spener (1635—1705), published a statement protesting the corrupt conditions of the state church in Germany. He expressed his "heartfelt desire for a God-pleasing reform" based upon "a more extensive use of the Word of God."[7] Spener realized that to merely hear the Word is not sufficient, but the Word should be digested and allowed to penetrate the inner man. To this end he said:

> Let it penetrate inwardly into your heart and allow the heavenly food* to be digested there, so that you get the benefit of its vitality and power.[8]

Later in his appeal he exhorts:

> Hence, it is not enough that we hear the Word with our outward ear, but we must let it penetrate to our heart....True prayer, and the best prayer, occurs in the inner man, and it either breaks forth in words or remains in the soul, yet God will find and hit upon it.[9]

2. AUGUST HERMANN FRANCKE

One of Spener's students, August Hermann Francke (1663—1727), followed him in calling the deadened church to a life of personal piety and devotion. Among Francke's students was the evangelist and Moravian Brethren leader, Count Nicholas Zinzendorf (1700—1760). Francke was diligent in reprinting the Scriptures in German, and in his introduction to one edition of Luther's translation he points to the "true joy and pleasure" to be found in prayerful reading of the Word:

> It is also reasonable that the reading of the Holy Scripture be done with all prayer and groaning, as well as praise and thanksgiving. For this is the

*See note A, p. 105.

simple way, that at all times one would have his good edification.[10]

It is also reasonable that the reading of the Holy Scripture be done with all prayer and groaning.

He then illustrates various ways to pray and read Genesis 1:1:

> For example: Gen. 1:1 "In the beginning God created the heavens and the earth."
>
> Oh, you eternal God, I thank you, that you teach me through your word from where the heavens and the earth have their origin.
>
> Or: Ah, dear Father in heaven, when I lift my eyes to the heavens, and look upon the earth, convey to my heart to muse this your divine word, that I should honor and worship you as the creator of the heavens and the earth.
>
> Or: Ah, dear God! have you created the heavens and the earth, then are you better and more glorious than the heavens and the earth. Thus, when I have only you, I will ask nothing after the heavens and the earth.
>
> Or: God, you surely are the Father over all that are called children in the heavens and the earth, who has created the heavens and the earth. Ah, teach me always to properly consider what a great Masterbuilder and Creator this piece of earth, my mortal body has.
>
> Or: Ah, dear Father in heaven, how can I be anxious any longer concerning the keeping of my body, as I call on you as my Father, who has created the heavens and the earth.[11]

Francke concludes by showing that this is the way to gain true pleasure in the Scripture:

> So one may remain at every little verse in the Bible and as Luther says, "Knock on every little twig, whether there would be some berries that would fall off." Should at the beginning one think it somewhat difficult and should the prayer not flow at once, one may go on, to try the same on another twig. If the soul is only hungry, the Spirit of God will not leave it undernourished. Yea, it will finally be found, that the man will see so many living fruit in one small verse, that he will remain there and settle, as under a tree richly laden. However, whosoever in the beginning is frightened by it, and considers it to be too difficult for him and he could not read the Scripture in this manner, it is his own fault, that during his entire life he never gains true joy and pleasure in the Scripture.[12]

In *A Guide to the Reading and Study of the Holy Scriptures* Francke sets forth his observations concerning the "simplest application of divine truth":

> The commencement of practical application is instituted with most ease, by including the text we are employed on and its component words, in short prayers or ejaculations, after its meaning has been properly ascertained. This method may appear simple and puerile; but many have approved its excellency by experience, and learned its value by the rich fruits which it has produced.[13]

He proposes that our meditation of the holy Scriptures be "tinged, as it were, with prayer, and exercised by the guidance of the Holy Spirit."[14]

> Nor ought you to be too anxious when you begin your meditations* on the Holy Scriptures; for if you join ardent prayers and a holy desire of knowing

*See note B, p.107.

Christ, to your reading of them, the matter will thereupon grow better, you will unawares be conducted by God himself into the most pleasant and sweet meditation of his eternal truth, and he will, by little and little, discover to you the inexhausted profundities and treasures of wisdom and knowledge, that are hid in Christ Jesus. (Col. 2:3.)[15]

REFERENCES

[1]William Perkins, *Treatise of Conscience* (Cambridge: University of Cambridge, 1606, reprinted, Amsterdam: Theatrvm Orbis Terrarvm Ltd., 1972), p. 297.

[2]*Ibid.,* p. 266.

[3]I. D. Thomas, comp., *The Golden Treasury of Puritan Quotations* (Chicago: Moody Press, 1975), p. 216.

[4]John Bunyan, "A Discourse Touching Prayer," *The Complete Works of John Bunyan,* ed. Henry Stebbing (New York: Johnson Reprint Corporation, 1970), vol. 1, p. 265.

[5]*Ibid.,* p. 265.

[6]*Ibid.,* p. 26.

[7]Phillip Jacob Spener, *Pia Desideria,* trans. Theodore G. Tappert (Philadelphia, PA: Fortress Press, 1964), pp. 29 and 87.

[8]*Ibid.,* p. 66.

[9]*Ibid.,* p. 117.

[10]August Hermann Francke, "August Hermann Francke's Kurzer Unterricht" *Die Bibel,* trans. William Jaques (Halle: Drud & Bertag, 1877), p. VI.

[11]*Ibid.,* p. IV.

[12]*Ibid.,* p. IV.

[13]August Hermann Francke, *A Guide to the Reading and Study of the Holy Scriptures,* trans. William Jaques (London: D. Jaques, 1813), p. 226.

[14]*Ibid.,* pp. 234-235.

[15]*Ibid.,* p. 235.

CHAPTER FIVE

II. THE RECORD OF CHURCH HISTORY (3)

E. The Testimony of the Evangelists

While the Puritans and the Pietists sought to bring the principles of the Word of God into the daily living of the believers, others such as John Wesley and George Whitefield committed themselves to bring the preaching of the Word out of the cathedrals and to the fields and street corners. They spent much of their lives traveling by horseback from village to village, where they preached to small home assemblies and large open-air gatherings.

1. JOHN WESLEY

The ministry of John Wesley (1703—1791) was built upon a life of discipline with constant attention to the reading of Scripture and prayer. One account from his journal demonstrates that it was his practice to mingle the Word with his prayer:

> Just as I began to pray, I was seized with such a cough that I could hardly speak. At the same time came strongly into my mind, "These signs shall follow them that believe" [Mark 16:17]. I called on Jesus aloud, to "increase my faith" [Luke 17:5], and to "confirm the word of His grace" [Acts 20:32]. While I was speaking, my pain vanished away, the fever left me, my bodily strength returned, and for many weeks I felt neither weakness nor pain. "Unto thee, O Lord, do I give thanks" [Psa. 75:1].[1]

In one of his letters regarding a profitable way to read, he encouraged reading the Old Testament in the morning and the New Testament in the evening. He then concluded that:

For all reading should be joined with meditation*
and prayer. Read a little, pray and meditate much.[2]

In the preface to his notes on the Old Testament, Wesley
offered practical help concerning the way to understand the
things of God:

Read a little,
pray and meditate much.

If you desire to read the Scriptures in such a manner as may most effectually answer this end, would
it not be advisable, (1) To set apart a little time, if
you can, every morning and evening for that purpose?...Serious and earnest prayer should be
constantly used before we consult the oracles of
God; seeing "Scripture can only be understood
through the same Spirit whereby it was given."[3]

2. GEORGE WHITEFIELD

George Whitefield (1714—1770) was known for his effective
outdoor evangelism in both Europe and America. In his private
life his usual practice was to read and pray over the Word of
God upon his knees, "a practice he started in college and continued all his life."[4] The following excerpts from his journals show
how he received nourishment and enjoyment from the Word:

My mind being now more open and enlarged, I began
to read the Holy Scriptures upon my knees, laying
aside all other books and praying over, if possible, every line and word. This proved meat indeed, and
drink indeed, to my soul.** I daily received fresh life,
light, and power from above. [I got more true knowledge from reading the Book of God in one month,
than I could *ever* have acquired from *all* the writings
of men].[5]

*See note B, page 107.
**See note A, page 105.

I followed my usual practice of reading and praying
over the Word of God upon my knees.[6]

...my usual practice of reading and praying over the Word of God upon my knees.

Other sections of Whitefield's journal show that when he
assimilated the Word by prayer he was enlightened and
strengthened:

> For many months have I been almost always upon
> my knees, to study and pray...and I have been di-
> rected, by watching and reading the Scripture in
> this manner, even in the minutest circumstances,
> as plainly as the Jews were, when consulting the
> Urim and Thummin at the High Priest's breast.[7]

> I immediately retired to my room, and kneeling
> down, with many tears, prayed, over that Psalm
> wherein David so often repeats these words—*"But
> in the Name of the Lord will I destroy them"* [Psa.
> 118:10-12].[8]

> On Sunday morning, I rose early,* and prayed over
> St. Paul's *Epistle to Timothy,* and more particularly
> over that precept, "Let no one despise thy youth"
> [1 Tim. 4:12].[9]

Even the Greek New Testament became the object of such
a practice:

> ...and the Greek Testament, every reading of which
> I endeavoured to turn into a prayer.[10]

> Though weak, I often spent two hours in my eve-
> ning retirements, and prayed over my Greek
> Testament.[11]

*See note C, page 110.

Howell Harris, one of Whitefield's co-laborers, testified in his diary concerning his contact with George Whitefield:

> He more mortified than me, sleeping for near a year 3 or 4 hours a night and kneeling on his knees all day long, reading and praying over the Scriptures.[12]

In Whitefield's sermons he encouraged his audience to turn God's Word into prayer:

> Do you also believe, and you shall be saved. Christ Jesus is the same now as He was yesterday, and will wash you in His own blood. Go home then, turn the words of the text into a prayer, and intreat the Lord to be *your* righteousness [Jer. 23:6]. Even so, come Lord Jesus, come quickly into all our souls! *Amen, Lord Jesus, Amen* and *Amen!* [Rev. 22:20].[13]

George Whitefield's ministry was fruitful because it was based on a foundation of God's Word and prayer. A century later George Müller of Bristol was provoked by Whitefield to lay the same foundation:

> Particularly was this impression deeply made on Mr. Müller's mind and heart: that Whitefield's un-paralleled success in evangelistic labours was plainly traceable to two causes and could not be separated from them as direct effects; namely, his *unusual prayerfulness, and his habit of reading the Bible on his knees.*[14]

3. JONATHAN EDWARDS

The preaching and writing of Jonathan Edwards (1703—1758) coupled with that of Whitefield sparked a spiritual awakening in the New England colonies. In his later years Edwards described his early contact with the Scripture:

> The first instance, that I remember, of that sort of inward, sweet delight in God and divine things, that I have lived much in since, was on reading those words, 1 Tim. 1:17. *Now unto the King*

eternal, immortal, invisible, the only wise God, be honour and glory for ever and ever, Amen. As I read the words, there came into my soul, and was as it were diffused through it, a sense of the glory of the Divine Being; a new sense, quite different from any thing I ever experienced before. Never any words of Scripture seemed to me as these words did. I thought with myself, how excellent a Being that was, and how happy I should be, if I might enjoy that God, and be rapt up to him in heaven, and be as it were swallowed up in him for ever! I kept saying, and as it were singing, over these words of scripture to myself; and went to pray to God that I might enjoy him, and prayed in a manner quite different from what I used to do; with a new sort of affection. But it never came into my thought, that there was any thing spiritual, or of a saving nature in this.[15]

F. The Testimony of the Missionaries

While men such as Wesley and Whitefield took the gospel to the common people, others such as David Brainerd, Henry Martyn, and Hudson Taylor spread the Word to nations and peoples who had never heard the good news.

1. DAVID BRAINERD

David Brainerd (1718—1747) reached out to the American Indians. He lived only twenty-nine years, but his journal published by Jonathan Edwards provoked countless men to "go into all the world." These excerpts from that journal show that his reading the Word issued in prayer and that the very language of his prayer came from the Word:

Afterward read the story of Elijah the prophet, 1 Kings, 17th, 18th, and 19th chapters; and also 2 Kings, 2d and 4th chapters. My soul was much moved, observing the faith, zeal, and power of that holy man; how he wrestled with God in prayer, &c. My soul then cried with Elisha, "Where is the Lord

God of Elijah!" O I longed for more faith! My soul breathed after God, and pleaded with him, that a "double portion of that spirit" which was given to Elijah, might "rest on me."[16]

...the very language which my soul uttered to God.

Afterward read from the 3d chapter of Exodus to the 20th, and saw more of the *glory* and *majesty of God* discovered in those chapters than ever I had seen before; frequently in the mean time falling on my knees and crying to God for the faith of Moses, and for a manifestation of the *divine glory*...The 15th chapter [of Exodus] seemed to be the very language which my soul uttered to God in the season of my first spiritual comfort.[17]

Just as Brainerd's times of reading were filled with prayer, so his times of prayer were filled with the Word:

The cry of my soul was, Psalm 65:3. "Iniquities prevail against me."[18]

My soul was sundry times in prayer enlarged for God's church and people. O that Zion might become the "joy of the whole earth!" [Psa. 48:2].[19]

Afterward, was enabled to pray fervently, and to rely on God sweetly, for "all things pertaining to life and godliness" [2 Pet. 1:3].[20]

Though in a very weak and low state, I enjoyed a considerable degree of comfort and sweetness in divine things; and was enabled to plead and use arguments with God in prayer, I think, with a child-like spirit. That passage of scripture occurred to my mind, and gave me great assistance, "If ye, being evil, know how to give good gifts to your children, how much more will your heavenly Father give the Holy Spirit to them that ask him?" [Luke 11:13]. This text I was helped to plead, and insist upon.[21]

On one occasion Brainerd described the sweetness of intermixing prayer with his meditation on John 7:37:

In the evening was much assisted in meditating* on that precious text, John, 7:37. "Jesus stood and cried," &c...I continued long in prayer and meditation, intermixing one with the other; and was unwilling to be diverted by any thing at all from so sweet an exercise.[22]

2. HENRY MARTYN

Prompted by the journal of Brainerd, Henry Martyn (1781—1812) took the Word of God to India and Persia. Like Brainerd, his life was short, a mere thirty-one years, but his influence was profound. The ministry of Henry Martyn was the fruit of combining God's Word with prayer:

By daily weighing the Scriptures, with prayer, he waxed riper and riper in his ministry. Prayer and the Holy Scriptures were those wells of salvation out of which he drew daily the living water for his thirsty immortal soul.[23]

By daily weighing the Scriptures, with prayer...

The editor of Martyn's journal described the difficulties of setting out for such a ministry and how Martyn was strengthened at such time by praying over the Scripture:

—By such considerations as these, by prayer— by reciting Scripture—by praying over it—by casting himself simply upon Christ—and by looking upon pain and suffering as his daily portion...Mr.

*See note B, page 107.

Martyn was carried through a season of great trib-
ulation.[24]

His journal shows that during his travels he practiced
combining reading and praying:

> Reading the Scriptures and prayer took up the first
> part* of the day.[25]

> Spent the first half of the day in reading the Scrip-
> ture and prayer.[26]

> Passed the day in reading and prayer, such as my
> prayers are.[27]

> I have read, or rather devoured, the four first chap-
> ters in the Hebrew Bible.[28]

In one account Martyn shows that he memorized Scripture so that it could serve as material for prayer:

> I began Isaiah, and learnt by heart the promises
> scattered through the twelve first chapters, hoping
> it may prove profitable matter for meditation** as
> well as prayer.[29]

3. HUDSON TAYLOR

About fifty years later, the gospel was brought to inland
China through the fruitful ministry of Hudson Taylor
(1832—1905). He described his experience of pleading the
Word in prayer:

> It was nearly two miles to Dr. Parker's and every
> moment appeared long. On my way thither, while
> wrestling mightily with God in prayer, the precious
> words were brought with power to my soul, "Call
> upon me in the day of trouble: I will deliver thee,
> and thou shalt glorify Me" [Psa. 50:15]. I was
> enabled at once to plead them in faith, and the
> result was deep, deep unspeakable peace and joy.[30]

*See note C, page 110.
**See note B, page 107.

4. JOHN HYDE

John Hyde (1865—1912), called by some "Praying Hyde," was faithful to take the Gospel to India. This account shows his practice of prayer mingled with the Word:

> Right on his face on the ground is Praying Hyde. This was his favorite attitude for prayer. Listen! he is praying; he utters a petition, and then waits; in a little time he repeats it, and then waits; and this many times until we feel that that petition has penetrated every fibre of our being and we feel assured that God has heard and without doubt He will answer. How well I remember him praying that we might open our mouth wide that He might fill it (Psalms 81:10). I think he repeated the word "wide" scores of times with long pauses between. "Wide, Lord, wide, open wide, wide." How effectual it was to hear him address God, "O Father, Father!"[31]

REFERENCES

[1]John Wesley, *The Journal of the Rev. John Wesley, A. M.,* ed. Nehemiah Curnock (London: Charles H. Kelly, 1909), vol. 2, p. 455.

[2]John Wesley, *The Letters of the Rev. John Wesley, A. M.,* ed. John Telford (London: The Epworth Press, 1931), vol. 6, p. 7.

[3]John Wesley, *A Compend of Wesley's Theology,* ed. Robert W. Burtner and Robert E. Chiles (New York: Abingdon Press, 1954), p. 22.

[4]John Lewis Gilmore, "Preparation: The Power of Whitefield's Ministry," *Christianity Today,* March 1980, p. 22.

[5]George Whitefield, *George Whitefield's Journals* (London: The Banner of Truth Trust, 1960), p. 60.

[6]*Ibid.,* pp. 86-87.

[7]*Ibid.,* p. 62.

[8]*Ibid.,* p. 38.

[9]*Ibid.,* p. 69.

[10]*Ibid.,* p. 56.

[11]*Ibid.,* p. 57.

[12]Arnold A. Dallimore, *George Whitefield* (London: The Banner of Truth Trust, 1971), vol. 1, p. 265.

[13]George Whitefield, *Selected Sermons of George Whitefield* (London: The Banner of Truth Trust, 1958), p. 500.

[14]Arthur T. Peirson, *George Müller of Bristol* (New York: Fleming H. Revell Company, 1941), p. 138.

[15]Jonathan Edwards, *Jonathan Edwards: Basic Writings,* ed. Ola Elizabeth Winslow (New York: New American Library, 1978), pp. 83-84.

[16]Jonathan Edwards, *The Life of Rev. David Brainerd* (New York: American Tract Society, 1833), p. 76.

[17]*Ibid.,* p. 77.

[18]*Ibid.,* p. 66.

[19]*Ibid.,* p. 79.

[20]*Ibid.,* p. 127.

[21]*Ibid.,* p. 304.

[22]*Ibid.,* p. 122.

[23]E. M. Bounds, *The Weapon of Prayer* (Grand Rapids, MI: Baker Book House, 1975), p. 133.

[24]John Sargent, Jr., *Memoir of the Rev. Henry Martyn,* B. D. (Boston, MA: Samuel T. Armstrong, and Crocker & Brewster, 1820), p. 130.

[25]*Ibid.,* pp. 202-203.

[26]*Ibid.,* p. 216.

[27]*Ibid.,* p. 261.

[28]*Ibid.,* p. 306.

[29]*Ibid.,* p. 133.

[30]Dr. and Mrs. Howard Taylor, *Hudson Taylor in Early Years* (London: Morgan and Scott, Ltd., 1911), p. 478.

[31]Francis McGaw, *Praying Hyde* (Minneapolis, MN: Bethany Fellowship, Inc., 1970), pp. 64-65.

Chapter Six

II. THE RECORD OF CHURCH HISTORY (4)

G. The Testimony of the Inner-life Writers

The writings of William Law and Andrew Murray hold a unique place in church history because of their emphasis on a personal and intimate relationship with the Lord. The Word and prayer were, they believed, vital and basic to such a relationship.

1. WILLIAM LAW

William Law (1686—1761) was widely known for his devotional writings, including *The Spirit of Prayer, The Spirit of Love,* and *A Serious Call to a Devout and Holy Life.* In *The Power of the Spirit* Law stressed the necessity of a present illumination by the Spirit in handling the Word of God:

> This is telling us in the plainest terms that it is just as essential for the Holy Spirit to reveal the truth of Scripture to the reader today as it was necessary for Him to inspire the writers thereof in their day....Therefore the Scriptures should only be read in an attitude of prayer, trusting to the inward working of the Holy Spirit to make their truths a living reality within us.[1]

Law encouraged us to give passages from the Word a place in our prayers:

> When...you meet with a passage that more than ordinarily affects your mind and seems as it were to give your heart a new motion towards God, you should try to turn it into the form of a petition, and then give it a place in your prayers.[2]

2. ANDREW MURRAY

Andrew Murray (1828—1917), the well-known Christian teacher of South Africa, spoke and wrote extensively about the believer's fellowship with the Lord. In his concern for the spiritual life of believers, he wrote that both the Word and prayer should be combined in the personal time spent with the Lord. This time spent in the "inner chamber" was for God and the believer to commune together:

> For intercourse with God, His Word and Prayer are both indispensable; and in the inner chamber they should not be separated. In His Word, God, speaks to me: in Prayer, I speak to God.[3]

Vitality for a life in Christ comes from prayer with God's Word as its base. Murray encourages us to turn the Word into prayer:

> How blessed would the inner chamber be, what a power and an inspiration in our worship, if we only took God's Word as from Himself, turning it into prayer, and definitely expecting an answer.[4]

If we only took God's Word as from Himself, turning it into prayer...

Heart-to-heart fellowship with the Lord, according to Murray, involves the interaction of God's Word and prayer:

> The Word comes from God's heart, and brings His thoughts and His love into my heart. And then the Word goes back from my heart into His great heart of love, and prayer is the means of fellowship between God's heart and mine.[5]

The Word is not only the content of the believer's prayer but the content of his life—of his being and of his actions. In *The Spirit of Christ,* Murray's classic work on the indwelling Spirit, he wrote:

God's Word must dwell in us richly; our faith must seek to hold it clearly and intelligently, and to plead it in prayer. To have the words of Christ abiding in us, filling life and conduct, is one of the secrets of acceptable prayer.[6]

How can a believer practice turning God's Word into prayer? In *The Prayer Life* Murray offered this practical advice for a profitable and powerful prayer life:

Read a few verses from the Bible. Do not concern yourself with the difficulties contained in them. You can consider these later; but take what you understand, apply it to yourself, and ask the Father to make His Word light and power in your heart. Thus you will have material enough for prayer from the Word which the Father speaks to you.[7]

3. HANNAH WHITALL SMITH

Hannah Whitall Smith (1832—1911) is widely known for her book on Christian living, *The Christian's Secret of a Happy Life*. In *Everyday Religion* she described the way to take the words of God:

If we will take the words of God, *i.e.,* His revealed truth, into our lips and eat it; that is, if we will dwell upon His words and say them over and over to ourselves, and thoroughly take in and assimilate their meaning in a common-sense sort of way, we shall find that our soul-life is fed and nourished by them,* and is made strong and vigorous in consequence.[8]

In *The God of All Comfort* she uses Psalm 23 as an example of praying the Word:

Then say the words over to yourself with all the will power you can muster, "The Lord is my Shepherd. He is. He is. No matter what I feel, He says

*See note A, page 105.

He is, and He is. I am going to believe it, come what
may." Then repeat the words with a different emphasis each time:

> The *Lord* is my Shepherd.
> The Lord *is* my Shepherd.
> The Lord is *my* Shepherd.
> The Lord is my *Shepherd.*[9]

H. The Testimony of the Brethren

Although the Bible had become increasingly accessible
to the believers since the time of Luther, it was mainly
through the Brethren during the last half of the nineteenth
century that so many of the truths of the Bible were opened.
The significance of Old Testament typology, the interpretation of the prophecies, and the fine meanings of the Hebrew
and Greek words were made clear. Concerning the Brethren,
W. H. Griffith Thomas said, "Among the children of God, it
was they who were most able to rightly divide the word of
truth"[10]:

1. JOHN NELSON DARBY

John Nelson Darby (1800—1882) is considered by many as
one of the foremost Bible expositors. While a leader among
the Brethren in England he wrote countless devotional and
doctrinal books as well as many hymns. In addition to his vol-
umes of expositions, he translated the Bible into German,
French, and English. As to the proper way to handle the Word
of God, he wrote:

Study the Bible
dear brother, with prayer.

Study the Bible, dear brother, with prayer. Seek
the Lord there, and not knowledge—that will come
too; but the heart is well directed in seeking the
Lord: the eye is single, and then the whole body is
full of light.[11]

2. GEORGE MÜLLER

George Müller's long life (1805—1898) was a testimony of prayer and faith. He believed that "you can never pray aright until He has spoken to you from His Word."[12] Thousands of recorded answers to prayers provided the sole means of raising up and supporting homes for many orphans. These two accounts give vivid testimony of his experience of mingling the Word with prayer:

> I began therefore to meditate* on the New Testament, from the beginning, early in the morning**....When thus I have been for a while making confession or intercession or supplication, or have given thanks, I go on to the next words or verse, turning all, as I go on, into prayer for myself or others, as the Word may lead to it, but still continually keeping before me that food*** for my own soul is the object of my meditation.[13]

> The Lord enabled me to put it to the test of experience, by laying aside commentaries, and almost every other book, and simply reading the Word of God and studying it. The result of this was that the first evening I shut myself into my room to give myself to prayer and meditation over the Scriptures, I learned more in a few hours than I had done during a period of several months previously....*But the particular difference was that I received real strength for my soul in doing so.*[14]

3. C. H. MACKINTOSH

C. H. Mackintosh (1820—1896) is most widely known for his *Notes on the Pentateuch*. In his *Notes on Genesis* he directs his readers to find Christ in the Word and feed on Him by faith:

> Points of truth however interesting, scriptural knowledge however profound and extensive, Biblical criticism however accurate and valuable, may

*See note B, page 107.
**See note C, page 110.
***See note A, page 105.

all leave the heart barren and the affections cold. We want to find Christ in the Word; and, having found Him, to feed on Him by faith.[15]

In a pamphlet, *Prayer and the Prayer Meeting,* he shows that our prayers are to be established on the Word of God:

The grand point for us is, to have an object laid upon our hearts by the Holy Ghost—an object as to which we can lay the finger of faith upon some distinct promise in the Word, and to persevere in prayer until we get what we want.[16]

He encouraged pleading the Scripture rather than being discouraged and in despair with the deadness around us:

What are we to do? Fold our arms in cold indifference? Give up in despair? Or give vent to complaining, murmuring, fretfulness, or irritation? God forbid! What then? Come together, "with one accord in one place;" get down on our faces before our God, and pour out our hearts, as the heart of one man, pleading Matthew 18:19.[17]

REFERENCES

[1] William Law, *The Power of the Spirit,* ed. Dave Hunt (Fort Washington, PA: Christian Literature Crusade, 1971), pp. 61-62.

[2] William Law, *Characters and Characteristics of William Law Nonjuror and Mystic,* ed. Alexander Whyte (London: Hodder and Stoughton, 1893), p. 158.

[3] Andrew Murray, *God's Best Secrets* (Westchester, IL: Good News Publishers, 1962), p. 25.

[4] *Ibid.,* p. 25.

[5] *Ibid.,* p. 25.

[6] Andrew Murray, *The Spirit of Christ* (Fort Washington, PA: Christian Literature Crusade, 1963), p. 135.

[7] Andrew Murray, *The Prayer Life* (Chicago, IL: Moody Press, n.d.), p. 77.

[8] Hannah Whitall Smith, *Everyday Religion* (Chicago, IL: Moody Press, 1893), p. 19.

[9] Hannah Whitall Smith, *The God of All Comfort* (New York: Fleming H. Revell Company, 1893), p. 58.

[10] Watchman Nee, *The Orthodoxy of the Church* (Anaheim, CA: Living Stream Ministry, 1994), p. 70.

[11] John Nelson Darby, *Letter of J. N. D.* (London: G. Morrish, 1914), vol. 2, p. 366.

[12] Stephen F. Olford, *Manna in the Morning* (Chicago, IL: Moody Press, n.d.), p. 11.

[13] W. Graham Scroggie, *Method in Prayer* (London: Pickering & Inglis Ltd., 1955), p. 18.

[14] Basil Miller, *George Müller Man of Faith and Miracles* (Minneapolis, MN: Bethany Fellowship, Inc., 1941), p. 21.

[15] C. H. Mackintosh, *Genesis to Deuteronomy* (Neptune, NJ: Loizeaux Brothers, 1972), p. 59.

[16] C. H. Mackintosh, *Prayer and the Prayer Meeting* (Addison, IL: Bible Truth Publishers, n.d.), p. 21.

[17] *Ibid.,* pp. 9-10.

CHAPTER SEVEN

II. THE RECORD OF CHURCH HISTORY (5)

I. The Testimony of the Evangelical Writers (1)

The evangelical writers during the nineteenth and the early twentieth centuries brought together much of what had been recovered over the previous centuries. Like the reformers they stood boldly upon the ultimate authority of the Scriptures; like the Pietists and the Puritans they emphasized a godly living rooted in Scripture reading and prayer; like the evangelists and the missionaries they promoted the preaching of God's Word as the gospel to all men; and like the inner-life writers and the Brethren they dug into the Word for light and nourishment.

1. EDWARD BICKERSTETH

The English evangelical minister, Edward Bickersteth (1786—1850), encouraged that we "read the Bible in the spirit of continual prayer."[1] In *A Help to the Study of the Scriptures* he suggested:

Turn passages of Scripture into prayer.

Prayer before you begin, prayer mixed with your reading, and prayer when you have done; fervent, earnest, and repeated entreaties for the help of the Holy Spirit to enlighten your mind, and bring home to your heart all that you read.[2]

To practice this he proposed:

Further: turn passages of Scripture into prayer: thus, when James says, Humble yourselves in the

sight of the Lord [James 4:10], pray in this way;
"O Lord God, grant that I may be humbled for my
many and great sins." Look up to God who can
alone give you this spirit of prayer.[3]

In *A Treatise on Prayer* he also points to the Word as the
basis of prayers:

Some have found it useful to take a Psalm, or a
chapter for a form of prayer; such as the 103d
Psalm for praise, the 51st Psalm for confession, the
9th of Daniel for intercession, the 12th of Romans
for petition.[4]

2. CHARLES G. FINNEY

The American evangelist, Charles G. Finney (1792—1875),
of the same period wrote in his *Memoirs* how during a period of
conflict he came to the Bible on his knees:

Often...I would go to my room and spend a long
time on my knees over my Bible. Indeed I read my
Bible on my knees a great deal during those days of
conflict, beseeching the Lord to teach me his own
mind on those points.[5]

3. ANDREW BONAR

Andrew Bonar (1810—1892), the Scottish reformer and
minister, enjoyed a long life of intimacy with the Lord. The
following excerpts from his journal provide a rare insight into
his private prayer life over a fifty-year period. The Word and
prayer were combined in his daily practice:

1835—In afternoon found myself much drawn out
in prayer and while singing verse 18 of Psalm 51.[6]

1835—My tendency to neglect or shorten prayer
and reading of Scripture, in order to hurry on to
study, is another subject of humiliation.[7]

1840—I find that reading much Scripture before-
hand is excellent preparation for prayer, and that
the time occupied is nothing in itself.[8]

1842—Passed six hours to-day...in prayer and Scripture reading.[9]

1846—Got comfort in prayer about this matter. Pled Isaiah 48:12: "I am the First and the Last," seeing the end from the beginning.[10]

Pled Isaiah 48:12.

1857—For nearly ten days past have been much hindered in prayer, and feel my strength weakened thereby. I must at once return through the Lord's strength to not less than three hours a day spent in prayer and meditation* upon the Word.[11]

1859—I prayed over and felt much, Job 40:4: "Behold! I am vile!"[12]

1870—By a singular providence, I have got special time to-day to fast and pray. In my ordinary reading of Scripture, I often get a single expression which serves as a key-note to my prayers, and sets my soul in order.[13]

1878—In the evening I spread out Dan. 10 before the Lord.[14]

1881—Prayed over Isaiah 11:2, 3 very specially.[15]

1890—More carefully than ever I hope this year to give two hours before going out every day, to meditate* on the Word and prayer. And in this way there shall go out of me *heavenward* "rivers of living water" that will bring down refreshing rain-showers.[16]

"Rivers of living water" will surely be the experience of those who, for so long a time, are diligent to labor over the Word through prayer.

4. ROBERT MURRAY McCHEYNE

Bonar's colleague, Robert Murray McCheyne (1813—1843), encouraged the use of the Bible in prayer. In a letter to a young

*See note B, page 107.

man, his counsel on "the best way of knowing the meaning of the Bible, and of learning to pray" was to:

> *Turn the Bible into prayer.* Thus, if you were reading the First Psalm, spread the Bible on the chair before you, and kneel, and pray, "O Lord, give me the blessedness of the man"; "let me not stand in the counsel of the ungodly." This is the best way of knowing the meaning of the Bible, and of learning to pray.[17]

Turn the Bible into prayer.

In a letter to John Trust in 1840 McCheyne wrote concerning the way "to conduct prayer-meetings" and promoted prayer that flows out of what is read in God's Word in the public prayer meeting:

> The prayer-meeting I like best, is where there is only praise and prayer, and the reading of God's Word....Pray in secret before going. Let your prayers in the meeting be formed as much as possible upon what you have read in the Bible. You will thus learn variety of petition, and a Scripture style.[18]

5. ROBERT GOVETT

Robert Govett's (1813—1901) extensive writings are marked by his faithfulness to biblical revelation. In *Entrance into the Kingdom* he acknowledged the need for prayer in the study of the Scriptures:

> But Christ's ministers now know his will, and understand his mysteries, only by study of the Scriptures with prayer for the Spirit's aid.[19]

6. JOSEPH BARBER LIGHTFOOT

Joseph Barber Lightfoot (1828—1889) was a "godly man, a teacher of pastors, and a preacher with a burden for lost souls."[20] He was regarded as the leading Greek scholar of his time. Bishop Lightfoot wrote on the flyleaf of his Greek New Testament:

> After all is said and done, the only way to know the Greek Testament properly is by prayer.[21]

7. BROOKE FOSS WESTCOTT

Brooke Foss Westcott (1825—1901), a close friend of Lightfoot, is principally recognized for his scholarly writing including detailed commentaries on portions of the New Testament. In his commentary on John 15:7 he wrote:

> *Ye shall ask what ye will]* According to the true reading, ask whatsoever ye will. The petitions of the true disciples are echoes (so to speak) of Christ's words. As He has spoken so they speak. Their prayer is only some fragment of His teaching transformed into a supplication, and so it will necessarily be heard.[22]

Their prayer is only some fragment of His teaching transformed into a supplication.

---

8. CHARLES HADDON SPURGEON

The reputation of C. H. Spurgeon (1835—1892), a diligent and powerful British minister during the last century, came at least in part, from his unique ability to use figurative language and dramatic illustrations in presenting the truths of God's Word. Spurgeon described the interdependence of God's Word and prayer using vivid illustrations:

> It is a great thing to pray one's self into the spirit and marrow of a text; working into it by sacred feeding thereon, even as the worm bores its way

into the kernel of the nut. Prayer supplies a leverage for the uplifting of ponderous truths.[23]

New veins of precious ore will be revealed to your astonished gaze as you quarry God's Word and use diligently the hammer of prayer.[24]

Use prayer as a boring rod, and wells of living water will leap up from the bowels of the Word. Who will be content to thirst when living waters are so readily to be obtained![25]

...as you quarry God's Word and use diligently the hammer of prayer.

In his book on Psalm 119, *The Golden Alphabet,* Spurgeon repeatedly emphasized the intimacy between the Word and prayer:

Divine commands should direct us in the subject of our prayers.[26]

"O that *my* ways were directed to keep thy statutes!" It were well if all who hear the word would copy this example and turn all that they hear into prayer.[27]

Let us each one say, *"Teach me thy statutes."* This is a sweet prayer for everyday use.[28]

The word of the Lord evidently arouses prayer.[29]

Let us always resort to prayer in our desponding times, for it is the surest and shortest way out of the depths. In that prayer let us plead nothing but the word of God; for there is no plea like a promise, no argument like a word from our covenant God.[30]

David had but few promises to quote, and many of these had been recorded in his own psalms, yet he pleads the word of the Lord; how much more should we do so, since to us so many holy men have spoken by the Spirit of the Lord in that wonderful library which is now our Bible! Seeing we have more promises, let us offer more prayers.[31]

Spurgeon exhorted those who desired to begin to be true readers of the Word: "You must get to your knees."[32] He viewed the Scripture as God's own writing for us to plead in prayer:

Every promise of Scripture is a writing of God, which may be pleaded before Him with this reasonable request: "Do as Thou hast said." The Creator will not cheat His creature who depends upon His truth; and, far more, the Heavenly Father will not break His word to His own child. "Remember the word unto Thy servant, on which Thou hast caused me to hope," is most prevalent pleading. It is a double argument: It is Thy Word, wilt Thou not keep it? Why hast Thou spoken of it if Thou wilt not make it good? Thou hast caused me to hope in it; wilt Thou disappoint the hope which Thou hast Thyself begotten in me?[33]

9. E. M. BOUNDS

Edward M. Bounds (1835—1913) "wrote transcendently about prayer, because he was transcendent in its practice."[34] For many years he prayed from four in the morning* until seven. His many books display "the depths of his marvelous research into the Life of Prayer."[35] Like Spurgeon, Bounds used figurative expressions to illustrate the role of the Word of God in prayer:

God's Word is the basis, as it is the directory of the prayer of faith.[36]

As this word of Christ dwelling in us richly is transmuted and assimilated, it issues in praying.[37]

The Word of God is the fulcrum upon which the lever of prayer is placed.[38]

*See note C, page 110.

His Word becomes the basis, the inspiration of our praying.[39]

The prayer of faith is based on the written Word.[40]

The Word of God is made effectual and operative, by the process and practice of prayer.[41]

The Word of God is the food, by which prayer is nourished and made strong.[42]

The Word of God is the food, by which prayer is nourished and made strong.

In *The Possibilities of Prayer,* he wrote specifically regarding the interdependence of the Word and prayer:

Prayer and the promises are interdependent. The promise inspires and energizes prayer, but prayer locates the promise, and gives it realization and location.[43]

In the same book he assessed prayer not based on the Word as shadowy, sandy, and fickle:

But prayer in its usual uniform and deep current is conscious conformity to God's will, based upon the direct promise of God's Word, and under the illumination and application of the Holy Spirit. Nothing is surer than that the Word of God is the sure foundation of prayer. We pray just as we believe God's Word. Prayer is based directly and specifically upon God's revealed promises in Christ Jesus. It has no other ground upon which to base its plea. All else is shadowy, sandy, fickle. Not our feelings, not our merits, nor our works, but God's promise is the basis of faith and the solid ground of prayer.[44]

In *The Necessity of Prayer,* he pointed emphatically to prayer not based on the Word as flabby, vapid, and void:

Unless the vital forces of prayer are supplied by God's

Word, prayer, though earnest, even vociferous, in its urgency, is, in reality, flabby, and vapid, and void. The absence of vital force in praying, can be traced to the absence of a constant supply of God's Word, to repair the waste, and renew the life.[45]

10. ALEXANDER WHYTE

Alexander Whyte (1837—1921) is regarded as the greatest Scottish preacher of his day. In *Lord, Teach Us to Pray* he emphasized the role of the Scriptures in pleading in prayer:

Tell Him: put Him in rememberance: search the Scriptures: collect the promises, and plead with Him to consider your case.[46]

Read the Parable of the Prodigal Son, and read nothing else: plead the Parable of the Prodigal Son, and plead nothing else,—till it is all fulfilled to you, and till you, and your house, are all made as merry as heaven itself.[47]

You must not charge God foolishly, till you have prayed, and pled, your way through that wonderful book [the book of Job].[48]

Only, oh learn to pray, and to plead. Study to pray. Study to plead. Give yourself to prayer. Pray without ceasing.[49]

11. DWIGHT L. MOODY

Dwight L. Moody (1837—1899) "was an untiring Bible student. He usually rose about daybreak* in summer, in order to have a quiet season alone with his Bible and his God, while his mind was fresh, and before the activities of the day divided his attention."[50] Moody encouraged his readers to have a time alone with God:

I never have seen a man or woman who spent fifteen or twenty minutes alone with God every day

---

*See note C, page 110.

that didn't have the dew all the while. I have never known one to backslide, either. You never get more than one day's journey from Christ if you come to Him every morning. Shut the world out. Get closeted with God and you will learn His secrets. I like to get up at five o'clock in the morning* and turn the key and be alone, and let God talk with me.

Some people say: "I cannot concentrate my thoughts. My mind just goes all over the world."

Well, that is true. There is no bigger tramp on the earth than the human mind. It is astonishing how the mind travels; and you ask, How can we bring our thoughts into captivity and have fellowship with God, instead of thinking of ourselves and everything under the sun?

Prayer is important, but there is something else as important. When I pray I am talking to God; when I read the Bible God talks to me. We need both....

The way to overcome impure thoughts is to fill the mind with better thoughts. You can do that by Bible study and prayer.[51]

In *Prevailing Prayer* he suggested the use of the Psalms as prayers:

...I do not know any better prayer that we can make than this prayer of David.

Let me call attention to that prayer of David, in which he says: "Search me, O, God, and know my heart; try me, and know my thoughts, and see if there be any wicked way in me, and lead me in the way everlasting!" [Psa. 139:23, 24]. I wish all my readers would commit these verses to memory. If we should all honestly make this prayer once every day there would be a good deal of change in our lives....I do not know any better prayer that we can make than this prayer of David....[52]

Later Moody suggested praying the words of another Psalm:

> Once again, let me call your attention to the prayer of David contained in the fifty-first Psalm. A friend of mine told me some years ago that he repeated this prayer as his own every week. I think it would be a good thing if we offered up these petitions frequently; let them go right up from our hearts.[53]

In introducing his book, *Prevailing Prayer: What Hinders It?* Moody wrote concerning the danger of separating the Word and prayer and pointed to the need to have the Word in order to pray acceptably:

> If we read the Word and do not pray, we may become puffed up with knowledge, without the love that buildeth up. If we pray without reading the Word, we shall be ignorant of the mind and will of God, and become mystical and fanatical, and liable to be blown about by every wind of doctrine.[54]

> The following chapters relate especially to Prayer; but in order that our prayers may be for such things as are according to the will of God, they must be based upon the revelation of His own will to us; for of Him, and through Him, and to Him are all things; and it is only by hearing His Word, in which we learn His purposes toward us and towards the world, that we can pray acceptably.[55]

12. ARTHUR T. PIERSON

A. T. Pierson (1837—1911) was an American missionary, writer, and widely respected Bible teacher. In one of his books, a biography of George Müller, Pierson describes how Müller began "to read the Word of God upon his knees"[56] and adds his own testimony to the value of such a practice:

Here we stop and ask what profit there can be in thus prayerfully reading and searching the Scriptures in the very attitude of prayer. Having tried it for ourselves, we may add our humble witness to its value.[57]

The Holy Scriptures will thus suggest the very words which become the dialect of prayer.

Pierson continued by describing how the words of the Bible become the dialect of prayer:

But perhaps the greatest advantage will be that the Holy Scriptures will thus suggest the *very words* which become the dialect of prayer. "We know not what we should pray for as we ought"—neither *what* nor *how* to pray. But here is the Spirit's own inspired utterance, and, if the praying be moulded on the model of His teaching, how can we go astray?...We turn precept and promise, warning and counsel into supplication, with the assurance that we *cannot be asking anything that is not according to His will* [1 John 5:14], for are we not turning His own word into prayer?[58]

Pierson's endorsement of such a habit continued:

The prayer habit, on the knees, with the Word open before the disciple, has thus an advantage which it is difficult to put into words: *It provides a sacred channel of approach to God.*[59]

Pierson also wrote a point-by-point defense of the Christian faith in which he described prayers that breathe a Scripture dialect:

But to-day, go where you will throughout the Christian world, and wherever Jesus Christ is known you will find those whose prayers to God and preaching to man, and whose very lives themselves, breathe a Scripture dialect.[60]

13. F. B. MEYER

F. B. Meyer (1847—1929), lifelong friend of D. L. Moody, was a tireless evangelist as well as the author of a number of devotional and interpretive books. In *Discover the Rich Life* he wrote:

ABOVE ALL, TURN FROM THE PRINTED PAGE TO PRAYER. If a cluster of heavenly fruit hangs within reach, gather it. If a promise lies upon the page as a blank check, cash it. If a prayer is recorded, appropriate it, and launch it as a feathered arrow from the bow of your desire. If an example of holiness gleams before you, ask God to do as much for you. If a truth is revealed in all its intrinsic splendor, entreat that its brilliance may ever irradiate the hemisphere of your life like a star. Entwine the climbing creepers of holy desire about the lattice work of Scripture. So shall you come to say with the Psalmist, *"Oh, how I love Thy law, it is my meditation all the day!"*[61]

Meyer, like A. T. Pierson and H. C. G. Moule encouraged kneeling while praying over the Word of God:

It is sometimes well to read over, on our knees, Psalm 119, so full of devout love for the Bible. And if any should chide us for spending so much time upon the Old Testament or the New, let us remind them of the words of Christ, *"Man shall not live by bread alone, but by every word that proceedeth out of the mouth of God* [Matt. 4:4]."[62]

14. H. C. G. MOULE

The writer of many spiritual and scholarly books, Handley C. G. Moule (1841—1920) was recognized because of his life of faith and his keen knowledge of the Bible. In his book,

Secret Prayer, he showed the Word of God to be the body and soul of prayer:

> Pre-eminent, supreme, among the helps to Secret Prayer I place of course the secret study of the holy written Word of God. Christian, who would indeed speak to God, you must indeed listen to the words of God, to the voice of God. Oh read the Bible, *learn* the Bible, with a view not merely to sermon, or to class, or again with a view to the mere doing of a religious duty, but now especially with a view to Secret Prayer. Read it on your knees, at least on the knees of your spirit. Read it to reassure, to feed, to regulate, to kindle, to give to your Secret Prayer at once body and soul. Read it that you may hold faster your certainty of being heard. Read it that you may know with blessed definiteness WHOM you have believed, and what you have in Him, and how He is able to keep your deposit safe. Read it in the attitude of mind in which the Apostles read it, in which the Lord read it. Read it, not seldom, to turn it at once into prayer. Open the twenty-fifth Psalm, or the hundred and nineteenth, or the Saviour's own High Priestly Prayer; and transmit petition after petition through your own soul to the Throne.[63]

REFERENCES

[1]E. Bickersteth, *A Help to the Study of the Scriptures* (Columbus, OH: I. N. Whiting, 1839), p. 107.

[2]*Ibid.,* p. 107.

[3]*Ibid.,* pp. 107-108.

[4]Edward Bickersteth, *A Treatise on Prayer* (Richmond, VA: Pollard & Converse, 1828), p. 63.

[5]Charles G. Finney, *Memoirs of Rev. Charles G. Finney* (New York: A. S. Barnes & Company, 1876), p. 54.

[6]Andrew A. Bonar, *Andrew A. Bonar, Diary and Letters,* ed. Majory Bonar (London: Hodder & Stoughton, 1894), p. 33.

[7]*Ibid.,* p. 34.

[8]*Ibid.,* p. 90.

[9]*Ibid.,* p. 98.

[10]*Ibid.,* p. 125.

[11]*Ibid.,* pp. 190-191.

[12]*Ibid.,* p. 199.

[13]*Ibid.,* p. 281.

[14]*Ibid.,* p. 327.

[15]*Ibid.,* p. 339.

[16]*Ibid.,* p. 379.

[17]Andrew W. Bonar, ed., *Memoirs of McCheyne* (Chicago, IL: Moody Press, 1947), pp. xix-xx.

[18]Robert Murray McCheyne, *The Works of Rev. Robert Murray McCheyne* (New York: Robert Carter & Brothers, 1873), p. 206.

[19]Robert Govett, *Entrance into the Kingdom* (Miami Springs, FL: Conley & Schoette Publishing Co., 1978), p. 97.

[20]Warren W. Wiersbe, *Listening to the Giants* (Grand Rapids, MI: Baker Book House, 1980), p. 48.

[21]*Ibid.,* p. 50.

[22]B. F. Westcott, *The Gospel according to St. John* (London: John Murray, 1908), p. 218.

[23]C. H. Spurgeon, *Lectures to My Students* (Grand Rapids, MI: Zondervan Publishing House, 1955), pp. 43-44.

[24]*Ibid.,* p. 44.

[25]*Ibid.,* p. 44.

[26]C. H. Spurgeon, *The Golden Alphabet* (Pasedena, TX: Pilgrim Publications, 1980), p. 32.

[27]*Ibid.,* p. 33.

[28]*Ibid.,* p. 50.

[29]*Ibid.,* pp. 71-72.

[30]*Ibid.,* p. 79.

[31]*Ibid.,* p. 207.

[32]C. H. Spurgeon, *The Infallibility of Scripture* (London: Metropolitan Tabernacle Pulpit, 1888, reprinted by Pilgrim Publications, Pasadena, TX), p. 629.

[33]Edward M. Bounds, *The Possibilities of Prayer* (New York: Fleming H. Revell Company, 1923), p. 24.

[34]Elgin S. Moyer, *Who Was Who in Church History* (Chicago, IL: Moody Press, 1962), p. 53.

[35]Edward M. Bounds, *Prayer and Praying Men* (Grand Rapids, MI: Baker Book House, 1979), p. 5.

[36]Edward M. Bounds, *The Necessity of Prayer* (Grand Rapids, MI: Baker Book House, 1976), p. 120.

[37]*Ibid.,* p. 120.

[38]*Ibid.,* pp. 120-121.

[39]*Ibid.,* p. 121.

[40]*Ibid.,* p. 121.

[41]*Ibid.,* p. 122.

[42]*Ibid.,* p. 123.

[43]Bounds, *The Possibilities of Prayer,* p. 18.

[44]*Ibid.,* pp. 22-23.

[45]Bounds, *The Necessity of Prayer,* p. 123.

[46]Alexander Whyte, *Lord, Teach Us to Pray* (Grand Rapids, MI: Baker Book House, 1976), p. 220.

[47]*Ibid.,* p. 221.

[48]*Ibid.,* p. 222.

[49]*Ibid.,* p. 225.

[50]William R. Moody, *The Life of Dwight L. Moody* (New York: Fleming H. Revell Company, 1900), p. 441.

[51]D. L. Moody, *Short Talks* (Chicago, IL: The Moody Press, 1900), pp. 111-112.

[52]D. L. Moody, *Prevailing Prayer* (Chicago, IL: Moody Press, n.d.), p. 33.

[53]*Ibid.,* p. 38.

[54]D. L. Moody, *Prevailing Prayer: What Hinders It?* (Chicago, IL: F. H. Revell Company, 1884), pp. 3-4.

[55]*Ibid.*, p. 4.

[56]Arthur T. Pierson, *George Müller of Bristol* (New York: Fleming H. Revell Company, 1941), p. 139.

[57]*Ibid.*, p. 139.

[58]*Ibid.*, p. 140.

[59]*Ibid.*, p. 140.

[60]Arthur T. Pierson, *The Gordian Knot* (New York: Funk & Wagnalls Company, 1902), p. 229.

[61]F. B. Meyer, *Discover the Rich Life* (Westchester, IL: Good News Publishers, 1964), p. 48.

[62]*Ibid.*, p. 48.

[63]H. C. G. Moule, *Secret Prayer* (London: Seeley and Co. Limited, 1893), pp. 40-42.

CHAPTER EIGHT

II. THE RECORD OF CHURCH HISTORY (6)

I. The Testimony of the Evangelical Writers (2)

15. A. B. SIMPSON

The messages and hymns of A. B. Simpson (1844—1919) continue to inspire the Lord's children. In one of his books he describes his early experience of prayer with a few others. Kneeling down with their Bibles opened they prayed according to the Word:

> I remember well the cold and desolate afternoon years ago, when a little band of humble, praying Christians met in an upper room to begin this work for God, and we opened our Bibles, and these words were just before us: "Who hath despised the day of small things?" [Zech. 4:10]. "Not by might, nor by power, but by my spirit, saith the Lord of hosts" [v. 6]. We knelt before Him there and thanked Him that we were poor, that we were few, that we were weak, and threw ourselves upon the might of the Holy Ghost, and He has never failed us.[1]

In *The Life of Prayer* Simpson encouraged us to appropriate God's promises by prayer:

> Happy are they who suspend their desires until they know their Father's will, and then, asking according to His will, they can rise to the height of His own mighty promise, "If ye abide in me, and my words abide in you, ye shall ask what ye will, and it shall be done unto you" [John 15:7]. "Thus saith the Lord,...Ask me of things to come concerning my

sons, and concerning the work of my hands command ye me" [Isa. 45:11]. What more can we ask of ourselves and others than that God's highest will, and that for us, shall be fulfilled?

How shall we know that will? At the very least, we may always know it by His Word and promise, and we may be very sure we are not transcending its infinite bounds if we ask anything that is covered by a promise of His Holy Word, but we may immediately turn that promise into an order on the very Bank of Heaven and claim its fulfillment by all the power of His omnipotence and the sanctions of His faithfulness.[2]

16. R. A. TORREY

Reuben A. Torrey (1856—1928), a diligent evangelist, wrote much concerning the Word and prayer. Such writing issued from his own experience of reading on his knees:

It is great to study the Bible on your knees.

God is ready to come down and meet us and talk with us face to face every time we open our Bibles. Oh, it is great to have God call you into His presence and say, "I have something I want to whisper right into your ear alone and into your heart," and then open your Bible and see God standing there and hear Him saying that which is written there in the Book before your eyes. Studying the Bible that way makes the Bible a new and living Book. It is great to study the Bible on your knees. It has been one of the rarest privileges of my life to read every chapter in the Bible and every verse in the Bible on my knees. And it is your privilege to do the same.[3]

In *How to Pray* he pointed to the Word as one of the secrets of prevailing prayer:

Here is one of the greatest secrets of prevailing prayer: To study the Word to find what God's will is as revealed there in the promises, and then simply take these promises and spread them out before God in prayer with the absolutely unwavering expectation that He will do what He has promised in His Word.[4]

In *How to Study the Bible for Greatest Profit* he wrote:

What new light often shines from an old familiar text as you bend over it in prayer! I believe in studying the Bible a good deal on your knees. When one reads an entire book through upon his knees—and this is easily done—that book has a new meaning and becomes a new book.

Prayer will do more than a college education to make the Bible an open and a glorious book.[5]

Torrey considered prayer and the study of the Word to be inseparable:

These two things, prayer and study of the Word of God, always go hand-in-hand, for there is no true prayer without study of the Word of God, and there is no true study of the Word of God without prayer.[6]

Study the Bible prayerfully. God, who is the author of the Bible, is willing to act as interpreter of it.[7]

In *The Baptism with the Holy Spirit* he warns of the dryness that comes from not handling the Word prayerfully.

God's power comes through prayer, it comes also through the Word (Ps. 1:2, 3; Josh. 1:8). Many have known the power that comes through the regular, thoughtful, prayerful, protracted meditation upon the Word, but business and perhaps Christian duties have multiplied, other studies have come in, the Word has been in a measure crowded out, and power has gone. We must meditate daily, prayerfully, profoundly upon the Word if we are to maintain power. Many a man has run dry through its neglect.[8]

17. JAMES M. GRAY

James M. Gray (1851—1935) was an excellent Bible teacher and an active evangelist. In his best known work, *How to Master the English Bible,* he pointed to prayerful reading:

> The most important rule is the last. Read it prayerfully. Let not the triteness of the observation belittle it, or all is lost. The point is insisted on because, since the Bible is a supernatural book, it can be studied or mastered only by supernatural aid.[9]

The conclusion of his plan for such mastery of the Bible is that our reading be punctuated with prayer:

> In the light of the foregoing, let the reader punctuate the reading of it and every part of it with prayer to its divine Author, and he will come to know "How to Master the English Bible."[10]

18. S. D. GORDON

S. D. Gordon (1859—1936) was the author of numerous devotional books including the *Quiet Talks* series. In *Quiet Talks on Prayer* he encouraged prayerful reading:

> *Read prayerfully.* We learn how to pray by reading prayerfully. This Book does not reveal its sweets and strength to the keen mind merely, but to the Spirit enlightened mind.[11]

In *Prayer and the Bible* he noted that our prayer takes on the color of our time in the Word:

> As we listen to His voice in His Word, and accept His promises, our praying will take on the colouration of our listening.

> Now Bible reading is the listening side of prayer. And the listening side controls the speaking side of prayer.[12]

19. W. H. GRIFFITH THOMAS

A minister, scholar, and teacher, W. H. Griffith Thomas

(1861—1924) showed the weakness of prayer life to be due to a lack of knowing God through His Word:

> God's Word is the fuel of our prayer. As we open the page in the morning, the promises prompt us to prayer, the examples incite us to prayer, the warnings urge us to prayer, the hopes of glory stir us to prayer—everything in the portion taken for our meditation* can be turned into prayer....Depend upon it, hiding God's Word in the heart is the secret of prayer, and the reason why our prayer-life is so weak and barren is that we do not know God through His Word.[13]

God's Word is the fuel of our prayer.

As to the connection between prayer and Bible study, he said:

> It is perhaps scarcely necessary to do more than call attention to the intimate and necessary connexion between prayer and all Bible study, whether the study be mainly critical or purely devotional. Bible knowledge is at once a cause and an effect of prayer. We need prayer for spiritual and intellectual enlightenment before and as we study the Word of God, while the results of our study will in turn lead to more prayer and increasing waiting on God in fellowship. Thus the two act and react on each other, for prayer in its simplest definition is just our speaking to God, and the Bible is God speaking to us.[14]

In *Grace and Power*, Thomas wrote:

> We must meditate on the Word of God. The food of the Scriptures, God's revelation of His will, is

*See note B, page 107.

needed to sustain prayer. The promises are to elicit prayer. The Word and prayer always go together, and no prayer is of use that is not based on, warranted by, and saturated with the Word of God.[15]

20. GEORGE W. TRUETT

George W. Truett (1867—1944) was a greatly loved and influential preacher and evangelist. His biographical account describes how, in the midst of crushing tragedy, he turned to desperate prayer mingled with the Word:

Day and night he read the Bible, especially the Psalms and Job and the closing chapters of the four Gospels....The early hours of Saturday night were spent in prayer and scripture reading. Over and over he could be heard saying: "My times are in thy hands" [Psa. 31:15].[16]

21. PETER AINSLIE

In *The Way of Prayer,* the American writer and editor, Peter Ainslie (1867—1943), wrote:

Hence, above all books, the Bible should be read until our reading becomes prayer.[17]

22. D. M. PANTON

D. M. Panton (1870—1955) wrote numerous pamphlets and books. He is best known for his writings on the Lord's return, the rapture, and the judgment seat of Christ. In his leaflet on prayer he wrote:

THE FOUNDATION OF PRAYER. The promises are colossal, and as sure as God Himself. Plead His own Word, and how shall God say nay?[18]

Pray *Scripturally.* Luke 11:1. To pray Scripture is a safe way to pray according to the will of God. Take pains to avoid a self-made liturgy. Prayers cease to leave the earth when they get caught in ruts.[19]

23. H. A. IRONSIDE

The effective ministry of Henry (Harry) A. Ironside
(1876—1951) was built upon help he received from an early
contact with Andrew Fraser:

> "Well," said the aged servant of the Lord, "sit
> down for a while and let's talk together about the
> Word of God." He then opened his much-worn Bible
> and for some time, in fact, until his strength was
> about gone, earnestly presented truth after truth of
> the precious Word of God, turning from one pas-
> sage to another. He did this in so simple and so
> sweet a manner that young Ironside entered into
> these truths in a way that he had never done be-
> fore. Tears began running down the cheeks of the
> young preacher.
>
> "Where did you get these things?" he asked. "Can
> you tell me where I can find a book that will open
> such wonderful truths to me? Did you learn these
> things in seminary?"
>
> He waited for Mr. Fraser's answer, which he
> never forgot, "My dear young man, I learned these
> things on my knees on the mud floor of a little sod
> cottage in the north of Ireland. There with my open
> Bible before me I used to kneel for hours at a time
> and ask the Spirit of God to reveal Christ to my
> soul and to open the Word to my heart. He taught
> me more on my knees on that mud floor than I ever
> could have learned in all the colleges or seminaries
> in the world."[20]

Ironside, who was described as one "saturated with the
Word of God,"[21] sought to stir each interested believer to
study the Bible for himself:

> What we get ourselves out of our Bibles in the pres-
> ence of God is worth far more than all that another
> passes on to us. We may learn from each other, but
> it is best to take nothing for granted; but, like Ruth
> the Moabitess, to "beat out that which we have

gleaned" [Ruth 2:17] through meditation and prayer.[22]

The book of Revelation according to Ironside, would cause us to appreciate Christ more through prayerful reading:

> If you would learn to appreciate Christ more, read this book, frequently and prayerfully.[23]

24. A. W. PINK

Arthur W. Pink (1886—1952) was one of the most prolific Christian writers of this century. In *Profiting from the Word* he describes the Word of God as "our directory in prayer."[24]

> Since we are required to "pray in the Spirit" (Jude 20), it follows that our prayers ought to be according to the Scriptures, seeing that He is their Author throughout.[25]

> In proportion as we hide the Word in our hearts, and it cleanses, moulds and regulates our inner man, will our prayers be acceptable in God's sight. Then shall we be able to say, as David did in another connection, "Of thine own have we given thee" (1 Chron. 29:14).[26]

In *Interpretation of the Scriptures* Pink encourages "a praying heart" in coming to the Word:

> The Word of God cannot be understood without a constant and laborious study, without a careful and prayerful scrutiny of its contents.[27]

> He must ever come to it in the spirit of prayer, crying "that which I see not teach Thou me" (Job 34:32).[28]

25. A. W. TOZER

A. W. Tozer (1897—1963) was a godly minister, scholar, and author. His prayer at the beginning of his ministry, which he later referred to as "the prayer of a minor prophet," was a prayer fully interwoven with the Word of God.

> Thou hast said, "I knew thee—I ordained thee—I sanctified thee," [Jer. 1:5] and Thou hast also said,

"Thou shalt go to all that I shall send thee, and
whatsoever I command thee thou shalt speak" [Jer.
1:7]. Who am I to argue with Thee or to call into
question Thy sovereign choice? The decision is not
mine, but Thine. So be it, Lord. Thy will, not mine,
be done.[29]

Tozer had a craving for communion with his Lord and gave
much time to prayerful study and avid feasting on the Scriptures, and he in turn encouraged others to read prayerfully:

To follow Christ is to carry a cross and the cross
is never easy. Read the two following passages
prayerfully, preferably on your knees: Exodus
23:20-33 and Isaiah 54.[30]

REFERENCES

[1]A. E. Thompson, *A. B. Simpson, His Life and Work* (Harrisburg, PA: Christian Publications, Inc., 1960), p. 88.

[2]A. B. Simpson, *The Life of Prayer* (Harrisburg, PA: Christian Publications, Inc., 1967), p. 22.

[3]R. A. Torrey, *The Importance and Value of Proper Bible Study* (Chicago, IL: Moody Press, 1921), pp. 47-48.

[4]R. A. Torrey, *How to Pray* (New York: Fleming H. Revell Company, 1900), p. 55.

[5]R. A. Torrey, *How to Study the Bible for Greatest Profit* (London: James Nisbet and Company Limited, 1903), pp. 112, 115.

[6]R. A. Torrey, *Great Pulpit Masters, R. A. Torrey* (New York: Fleming H. Revell Company, 1950), vol. 3, pp. 158-159.

[7]R. A. Torrey, *How to Succeed in the Christian Life* (New York: Fleming H. Revell Company, 1906), p. 61.

[8]R. A. Torrey, *The Baptism with the Holy Spirit* (Chicago, IL: The Bible Institute Colportage Association, 1943), p. 65.

[9]James M. Gray, *How to Master the English Bible* (Chicago, IL: The Winona Publishing Company, 1904), p. 52.

[10]*Ibid.,* p. 55.

[11]S. D. Gordon, *Quiet Talks on Prayer* (New York: Grosset and Dunlap, 1941), p. 166.

[12]S. D. Gordon, *Prayer and the Bible* (New York: Fleming H. Revell Company, 1935), p. 15.

[13]W. H. Griffith Thomas, *Life Abiding and Abounding* (Chicago, IL: The Bible Institute Colportage Association, nd.), p. 15.

[14]W. H. Griffith Thomas, *Methods of Bible Study* (London: Marshall, Morgan & Scott, Ltd., n.d.), p. 117.

[15]W. H. Griffith Thomas, *Grace and Power* (Grand Rapids, MI: Wm. B. Eerdmans Publishing Company, 1949), p. 122.

[16]Powhatan W. James, *George W. Truett* (Nashville, TN: Broadman Press, 1940), pp. 87-88.

[17]Peter Ainslie, *The Way of Prayer* (New York: Fleming H. Revell Company, 1924), p. 107.

[18]D. M. Panton, *Prayer* (London: Chas. J. Thynne, n.d.), p. 1.

[19]*Ibid.,* p. 2.

[20]E. Schuyler English, *Ordained of the Lord, H. A. Ironside* (Neptune, NJ: Loizeaux Brothers, 1976), p. 94.

[21]Warren W. Wiersbe, *Listening to the Giants* (Grand Rapids, MI: Baker Book House, 1980), p. 198.

[22]H. A. Ironside, *Lectures on the Book of Revelation* (Neptune, NJ: Loizeaux Brothers, 1920), p. 11.

[23]*Ibid.*, p. 8.

[24]A. W. Pink, *Profiting from the Word* (Carlisle, PA: The Banner of Truth Trust, 1970), p. 46.

[25]*Ibid.*, p. 46.

[26]*Ibid.*, p. 46.

[27]A. W. Pink, *Interpretation of the Scriptures* (Grand Rapids, MI: Baker Book House, 1980), p. 23.

[28]*Ibid.*, p. 23.

[29]David J. Fant, *A. W. Tozer, a Twentieth Century Prophet* (Harrisburg, PA: Christian Publications, Inc., 1964), p. 17.

[30]*Ibid.*, p. 80.

NOTES

Note A

THE WORD AS NOURISHMENT

Closely related to the awareness of the vital relationship between the Word and prayer is the realization of the function of the Word "to impart God into us as life and as the nourishment of life."[1] *"Thy words were found, and I did eat them; and thy word was unto me the joy and rejoicing of mine heart"* (Jer. 15:16a).

In *Grace and Power* W. H. Griffith Thomas writes concerning the scriptural revelation of the "food of the Word of God."[2] He points to four aspects of the Word as food to us:

> The "good food" is, of course, the food of the Word of God, for as food builds up the tissues of the body, repairs waste, and preserves us in health, so the Word of God is the complete food of the soul. It is noteworthy that we have it brought before us in the Bible [1] as milk for babes [1 Pet. 2:2-3; 1 Cor. 3:2], [2] as strong meat for adults [Heb. 5:14], affording us the necessary constituents of spiritual nutrition, and [3] as honey [Psa. 19:10; 119:103; Ezek. 2:9—3:3], suggesting the pleasure and enjoyment of dessert in addition to [4] the food actually necessary for life and work [Jer. 15:16; Job 23:12b; 1 Tim. 4:6].[3]

Watchman Nee (1901—1972), whose words are a source of revelation and supply to believers throughout the world, wrote in *The Christian* regarding receiving nourishment from the Word of God:

We should not read the Scriptures in a casual way,
but use prayer and meditation to digest the word of
God.[4]

Witness Lee (1905—1997), a co-worker of Watchman Nee
in China, delivered and published several thousand messages
related to the believers' enjoyment and experience of Christ.
In *A Time with the Lord* he encourages touching the Word of
God for nourishment and enjoyment:

> In the New Testament, the Lord Jesus speaks of
> God's Word as spiritual food: "But He answered
> and said, It is written, Man shall not live on bread
> alone, but on every word that proceeds out through
> the mouth of God" (Matt. 4:4). Every word which
> proceeds out of the mouth of God is spiritual food to
> nourish us. The Scriptures reveal at least three
> cases of those who ate the Word of God. One is Jer-
> emiah, who said, "Your words were found and I ate
> them..."(Jer. 15:16)...Jeremiah *ate the word of God.*
> *This means he received the Word into him, assimi-*
> *lated it, and made it a part of himself.*
>
> In the same verse Jeremiah also said, "Your
> word became to me the joy and rejoicing of my
> heart." This is a kind of enjoyment. The Word, after
> being eaten, became a joy and also a rejoicing. Joy
> is experienced within, and rejoicing is expressed
> without. God's Word is an enjoyment; after being
> taken into us and assimilated into our very being,
> it becomes joy within us and rejoicing without.
>
> There are also a number of other verses which
> reveal this same thought to us. David said, "How
> sweet are thy words unto my *taste!* yea, sweeter
> than honey to my mouth" (Psa. 119:103). The Word
> is an enjoyment, and it is even sweeter and more
> pleasant than honey to our taste. From all these
> verses we realize that the Word of God is not only
> for us to learn, but more for us to taste, to eat, to
> enjoy, and to digest.

Then in 1 Peter 2:2-3 we see that to eat the Word is to taste the Lord. "As newborn babes, long for the guileless milk of the word in order that by it you may grow unto salvation, if you have *tasted* that the Lord is good." In verse 2 there is the eating of the Word, and in verse 3, the tasting of the Lord. When we eat the Word of God as our spiritual nourishment, we taste the Lord.

Another important verse is 1 Timothy 4:6b: "You will be a good member of Christ Jesus, *being nourished* with the words of the faith."...the concept of the apostle Paul was that God's Word is food to nourish God's children. We must be nourished in the Word, not merely taught. Praise the Lord, nourished! Hallelujah, we must be nourished with the Word, not just taught with letters! Paul's emphasis is not that we should be taught with knowledge, but that we should be nourished with the riches of the Word.[5]

Note B

MEDITATING ON GOD'S WORD

Many of the quotations included in this collection use the term "meditate." This is based on numerous Old Testament verses. As used there "it involves a musing and speaking and while often distinguished from prayer, as with Origen, 'meditation on the Scriptures often passes into prayer.'"[6]

Joshua was charged by the Lord to meditate in the book of the law day and night. "This book of the law shall not depart out of thy mouth; but thou shalt meditate therein day and night, that thou mayest observe to do according to all that is written therein" (Josh. 1:8). According to John Anderson in *Searching the Scriptures,* the word *meditate* in this verse is "from a Hebrew word [*hagah*] meaning to 'murmur' or 'mutter' hence, to speak with oneself, murmuring in a low voice, as is often done by those who are musing."[7]

William Wilson's *Old Testament Word Studies* points to the other uses of this Hebrew word in the Old Testament which indicate that the practice of meditating involves a kind of speaking and not merely a silent pondering:

> To murmur, to mutter; to make sound with the mouth; it is thus generally applied to the roaring of the lion when he has got his prey, Isa. 31:4; to soft thunder, Job 37:2; to the muttering of charmers, Isa. 8:19; to the sound of the harp, Ps. 9:16, 42:3; to the mourning of the dove, Isa. 38:14, 59:11; to the groaning and sighing of men, Isa. 16:7, Jer. 48:31. It is from the palate, Prov. 8:7; the throat, Ps. 115:7; or the tongue, Ps. 35:28. When understood, therefore, of meditation, it implies what we express by one talking to himself.[8]

In the Psalms another Hebrew word is translated *meditate*. The psalmist in Psalm 119 speaks of meditation in the statutes and precepts. "I will meditate in thy precepts" (v. 15); "Thy servant did meditate in thy statutes" (v. 23); "I will meditate in thy statutes" (v. 48); "I will meditate in thy precepts" (v. 78); "O how I love thy law! it is my meditation all the day" (v. 97); "Thy testimonies are meditation" (v. 99); and "Mine eyes prevent the night watches, that I might meditate in thy word" (v. 148). Here the Hebrew word [*siyach*] indicates a kind of speaking and "talk with oneself." Meditate in these verses indicates a slow and fine exercise over the Word.

In *Life-study of Psalms* Witness Lee describes his experience of musing on the word early in the morning:

> In several verses the writer of Psalm 119 tells us that he mused upon God's word (vv. 15, 23, 48, 78, 99, 148). To muse on the word is to taste it through careful considering. Thus, musing is a kind of enjoyment. I can testify that most of the enlightenment I receive comes by musing on the Word early in the morning. As I muse on the Word, I think about it with much consideration in a detailed way.[9]

S. D. Gordon describes the meaning of the word *meditate* as a repetitious muttering, a ruminating:

Run through and pick out this word with its varia-
tions. The word underneath that English word
means to mutter, as though a man were repeating
something over and over again, as he turned it over
in his mind. We have another word, with the same
meaning, not much used now—ruminate. We call
the cow a ruminant because she chews the cud. She
will spend hours chewing the cud, and then give us
the rich milk and cream and butter which she has
extracted from her food. That is the word here—
ruminate. Chew the cud, if you would get the rich-
est cream and butter here.[10]

Witness Lee in *Life-study of Leviticus* uses the same ter-
minology:

Chewing the cud signifies receiving the word of
God with much consideration and reconsideration.
Just as a cow chews its cud, we should consider and
reconsider the word of God. We may do this while
we pray-read early in the morning. As we are
pray-reading, we may consider and reconsider the
word. This is to chew the cud to receive nourishment by reconsidering what we receive from God's
word.[11]

A. W. Tozer encouraged the practice of the art of prayerful
Bible meditation:

Let the old saints be our example. They came to the
Word of God and meditated. They laid the Bible on
the old-fashioned, handmade chair, got down on
the old scrubbed, board floor and meditated on the
Word. As they waited, faith mounted. The Spirit
and faith illuminated. They had only a Bible with
fine print, narrow margins and poor paper, but
they knew their Bible better than some of us do
with all of our helps....Let us just be plain,
thoughtful Christians. Let us open our Bibles,
spread them out on a chair, and meditate on the
Word of God. It will open itself to us, and the Spirit

of God will come and brood over it....I do challenge you to meditate, quietly, reverently, prayerfully, for a month. Put away questions and answers and the filling in of blank lines in the portions you haven't been able to understand. Put all of the cheap trash away and take the Bible, get on your knees, and in faith, say, "Father, here I am. Begin to teach me!"[12]

Note C

EARLY RISING

Many of the quotations include references to praying over the Bible early in the day. Indeed, the best time for a personal practice of pray-reading the Word is early in the morning. In *Prevailing Prayer* Taylor G. Bunch encourages morning watch:

> The early morning is the best time for study and prayer....To the Lord should be given our first time and thoughts in the day. He should be the first person to whom we speak in the morning, and we should permit Him to be the first to speak to us. This is the best way to begin the day. It is the way Jesus began His days.
>
> Luther said, "If I fail to spend two hours in prayer each morning, the devil gets the victory through the day. I have so much business I cannot get on without spending three hours daily in prayer." Luther always combined prayer with the study of the Word. He said further, "He that has prayed well has studied well. Prayer is the better half of study."
>
> Wesley devoted the morning hours from four to six in prayer, meditation, and study....Charles Simeon [1759—1836] devoted the hours from four to six each morning to God. Bishop [Francis] Asbury [1745—1816] said, "I purpose to rise at four o'clock as often as I can and spend two hours in prayer and meditation." Samuel Rutherford [c. 1600—1661] rose at three for his prayer appointment with God.[13]

Watchman Nee in *Messages for Building Up New Believers* encourages the new believers to rise early to 1) fellowship with God, 2) praise and sing, 3) read the Bible, and 4) pray:

> Those who rise up early in the morning reap much spiritual benefit. Their prayers at other times of the day cannot be compared with their prayers in the early morning. Their Bible reading at other times of the day cannot be compared with their reading in the early morning....Read a single portion of the Bible carefully, always mingling your reading with unceasing communion with God and singing.[14]

While speaking at the Keswick Convention, H. B. Macartney from Australia, speaking out of his own "life of intense devotion to the person of the Lord Jesus and a practice of private prayer," entreated his listeners:

> I want to entreat you to get up a little earlier than you have been in the habit of doing every morning, and to meet God over His Word. You sometimes, perhaps, have tried prayer by itself, and found it rather dull and heavy. You have tried the Word of God by itself, and got a little drowsy over it. Now mingle the two together, and while you read, pray; and while you pray, praise, and then you will have a blessed hour with God.[15]

Note D

PRAY-READING

In the May and August 1967 issues of *the Stream* Witness Lee introduced his readers to the term "pray-reading":

> Suppose we do agree to spend more time daily in the presence of the Lord, what shall we do? We must learn to do only one thing—that is, we must mingle our reading with our praying. We must contact the Lord by mingling our reading with prayer, and by mingling our prayer with reading. This is

why I have used a new word, "pray-read." We must pray-read the Word.

First, begin by spontaneously offering a short prayer to the Lord. Then open your Bible and start to read. While you are reading, spontaneously respond to the Lord with what you read....Simply read and pray, pray and read—pray-read. In this way, your praying will be mingled with your reading. Read and pray, read and pray, then pray more and read again.[16]

In *Pray-reading the Word* he encourages pray-reading as the proper way to come to the Word:

Having seen that the Word of God is the very essence of God Himself and that it is for our spiritual enjoyment and nourishment, we must now see the proper way to come to the Word. What is it? We must look at the Word of God as recorded in Ephesians 6:17-18: "Receive...the sword of the Spirit, which Spirit is the Word of God." It is the Spirit that is the Word of God. Then verse 18 continues: "By means of all prayer and petition." The verses then together are: "Receive...the sword of the Spirit, which Spirit is the word of God, by means of all prayer and petition." In what way are we to take the Word of God according to this passage? By means of all prayer and petition. This is what we call *pray-reading!* Again, we must repeat—the Word of God must be taken by means of all prayer.[17]

In the same booklet he encourages pray-reading with others:

For more enjoyment and nourishment and to pray-read the Word properly and adequately, we need the Body, the church. We may enjoy pray-reading the Word privately, but if we try it with a group of other Christians, we will be in the third heavens!...The best way to pray-read is with other members of the Body. You will profit by pray-reading alone, but you will see the difference when you come together with other brothers and sisters....If you will try this both privately and corporately, you will be able to testify of the riches of Christ that have been imparted to you by pray-reading the Word of God. You will see blessing and growth in your spiritual life.[18]

Now to enjoy Thee I come to Thy Word,
On Thee to feed till my hunger is o'er.
Now in my spirit I turn unto Thee,
Of Thee to drink till I'm thirsty no more.

Feeding and drinking, Lord Jesus, of Thee,
Feeding by reading, and drinking by prayer;
Reading and praying, I eat and I drink,
Praying and reading—Lord, Thou are my fare.[19]

REFERENCES

[1]Witness Lee, "The Nature and Function of the Word," *the Stream,* vol. 5, no. 3; August 1, 1967 (Los Angeles, CA: The Stream Publishers), p. 5.

[2]W. H. Griffith Thomas, *Grace and Power* (New York: Fleming H. Revell Company, 1916), p. 154.

[3]*Ibid.,* p. 154.

[4]Watchman Nee, *The Christian* (Anaheim, CA: Living Stream Ministry, 1992), p. 70.

[5]Witness Lee, *A Time with the Lord* (Anaheim, CA: Living Stream Ministry, 1991), pp. 5-8.

[6]Etienne Gilson, *The Mystical Theology of Saint Bernard,* trans., A. H. C. Downes (New York: Sheed and Ward, 1940), p. 18.

[7]John Anderson, *Searching the Scriptures* (London: Morgan and Scott, 1878), p. 25.

[8]William Wilson, *Old Testament Word Studies* (Grand Rapids, MI: Kregel Publications, 1978), p. 271.

[9]Witness Lee, *Life-study of Psalms,* (Anaheim, CA: Living Stream Ministry, 1991), p. 461.

[10]S. D. Gordon, *Quiet Talks on Prayer* (New York: Grosset and Dunlap, 1941), p. 107.

[11]Witness Lee, *Life-study of Leviticus* (Anaheim, CA: Living Stream Ministry, 1991), p. 315.

[12]A. W. Tozer, *The Tozer Pulpit,* comp. Gerald B. Smith (Harrisburg, PA: Christian Publications, Inc., 1968), vol. 2, p. 117.

[13]Taylor G. Bunch, *Prevailing Prayer* (Washington, D.C.: Review and Herald, 1946), pp. 46-47.

[14]Watchman Nee, *Messages for Building Up New Believers* (Anaheim, CA: Living Stream Ministry, 1994) pp. 166, 169-170.

[15]H. B. Macartney, "Christ the Cleanser," *Keswick's Authentic Voice,* Herbert F. Stevenson, ed. (Edinburgh: Marshall, Morgan & Scott, 1959), pp. 174-175.

[16]Witness Lee, "How Christ Can Be Our Enjoyment," *the Stream,* vol. 5, no. 2; May 1, 1967 (Los Angeles, CA: The Stream Publishers), p. 14.

[17]Witness Lee, *Pray-reading the Word* (Anaheim, CA: Living Stream Ministry, 1991), p. 8.

[18]*Ibid.,* pp. 12-14.

[19]Witness Lee, *Hymns* (Los Angeles, CA: Living Stream Ministry, 1988), p. 740-741.

INDEX